HOW TO USE

The Internet

Fourth Edition

HOW TO USE

The Internet
Fourth Edition

Mark H. Walker

Ziff-Davis Press
An imprint of Macmillan Computer Publishing USA
Emeryville, California

Acquisitions Editor	Juliana Aldous
Editor	Barbara Dahl
Technical Reviewer	Trudy Reisner
Project Coordinator	Carol Burbo
Proofreader	Timothy Loughman
Book Design	Dan Armstrong and Bruce Lundquist
Page Layout	M. D. Barrera
Indexer	Carol Burbo

Ziff-Davis Press imprint books are produced on a Macintosh computer system with the following applications: FrameMaker®, Microsoft® Word, QuarkXPress®, Adobe Illustrator®, Adobe Photoshop®, Adobe Streamline™, MacLink®Plus, Aldus® FreeHand™, Collage Plus™.

Ziff-Davis Press, an imprint of
Macmillan Computer Publishing USA
5903 Christie Avenue
Emeryville, CA 94608

ISBN 1-56276-560-4

Manufactured in the United States of America
10 9 8 7 6 5 4 3

This book was produced digitally by Macmillan Computer Publishing and manufactured using computer-to-plate technology (a film-less process) by GAC/Shepard Poorman, Indianapolis, Indiana.

THIS BOOK IS DEDICATED TO Batman, Mike Schmidt, Ayrton Senna, Jim Clark, Lumiere, Spiderman, minor league baseball, the 1980 U.S.A. Olympic hockey team, the Eagles, my wife, Toad the Wet Sprocket, the Gin Blossoms, my children, Def Leppard, the Crew of Apollo 13, green deciduous trees, the Crew of the Mir, a kid's imagination, George Bush, Junior Seau, Thumbelina, Colin Powell, Ray Kinsella, blue and yellow Lola T-342s, miniskirts, ice cold Coronas (with lime), a Panama City sunset, a California desert sunrise, a summer thunderstorm in Henry, Michael Jordan, Lynn St-James, David Drake, the good in all of us, and that first cup of coffee in the morning.

THANKS to Juliana Aldous, friend and editor, for giving me the work. Thanks to Barbara Dahl for the information, advice, and top-notch edit.

Most of all thanks to my wife, Janice—the screen shots and layout ideas were her doing—and my girls, Denver, Jessica, and Ayron: My sanity and generally positive disposition is their doing.

T A B L E

Introduction   xi

PART 1

Understanding the Internet

What Is the Internet?   2

How the Internet Works   4

What Is the World Wide Web?   6

How the World Wide Web Works   8

How to Read URLs   10

What Is E-Mail?   12

What Are Newsgroups?   14

○ ⓕ ⓒ ⓞ ⓝ ⓣ ⓔ ⓝ ⓣ ⓢ

PART 2

Hooking Up

The Hardware You Need to Access the
Internet   18

How Your Modem Works   20

How to Choose a Local Internet Service
Provider   22

How to Install Netscape Navigator   24

How to Configure Navigator   26

How to Install Internet Explorer   28

How to Configure Internet Explorer   30

Installing Online Services   32

How to Dial In   34

PART 3

Using the Browser

How to Display Web Pages   38

How to Navigate among Web Pages   40

How to Navigate Frames on a Page   42

How to Use Netscape Navigator
Bookmarks   44

How to Set an Internet Explorer
Favorite   46

How to Update Your Favorites and
Bookmarks Automatically   48

How to Listen to the Web with
RealAudio   50

How to Watch Web Movies with
QuickTime   52

How to Use the Internet as a Phone   54

PART 4

Searching the Web

Web Search Engines   58

How to Find Search Tools and Navigation
Aids   60

How to Use Yahoo!   62

How to Use Lycos   64

How to Use InfoSeek   66

How to Use AltaVista   68

How to Use Excite   70

How to Use AOLNetFind   72

How to Use HotBot   74

PART 5

Using the Internet

How to Save and Print a Web Page   78

How to Download a Program   80

How to Install Downloaded Files   82

What Is FTP?   84

How to Connect to an FTP Site   86

How to Navigate in an FTP Site   88

How to Download Files from an
FTP Site   90

How to Upload a File to an FTP Site   92

What Is Telnet?   94

How to Set Up Netscape Navigator to Use
Telnet   96

How to Connect to a Telnet Site   98

How to Navigate in a Remote Application 100

What Are Gopher Sites? 102

Visiting a Gopher Site 104

PART 6

Security on the Internet

Security Issues on the Internet 108

Visiting a Secure Web Site 110

Downloading and Installing PGP 112

How to Send Secure Messages 114

How to Download and Install Security Certificates 116

How Companies Maintain Security 118

How to Shop on the Internet 120

How to Find Shopping Areas on the Web 122

How to Download and Install CyberPatrol 124

How to Download and Install Net Shepherd 126

How to Find Other Net-Filtering Programs 128

How to Protect Your Computer from Viruses 130

How to Get Comfortable with Cookies 132

PART 7

E-Mail and Internet Communities

How to Send E-Mail with Netscape Mail 136

How to Send E-Mail with Microsoft Exchange 138

How to Handle Incoming E-Mail Messages 140

How to Store E-Mail Addresses 142

How to Reply to or Forward an E-Mail 144

How to Attach a File to Your E-Mail 146

How to Attach Multiple Files 148

How to Save and Unzip an Attachment 150

How to Choose a Mailing List 152

How to Subscribe to a Mailing List 154

What Are Newsgroups? 156

How to Search Newsgroups with Deja News 158

How to Subscribe to a Newsgroup 160

How to Read Newsgroup Messages 162

How to Interact with Newsgroups 164

How to Post a Newsgroup Message 166

How to Chat with IRC 168

How to Use the Proper Chat Etiquette 170

How to Use Voice-Aided Chat   172

How to Game on the Internet   174

Joining an Online Game Service   176

How to Use MUDs   178

PART 8
New Technologies and Software

How to Download Netscape
Communicator   182

How to Install Communicator   184

How to Configure Communicator   186

How to E-Mail with Communicator   188

How to Access Newsgroups with
Communicator   190

How to Use Other Communicator
Features   192

How to Download Internet
Explorer 4.0   194

How to Install Internet Explorer 4.0   196

How to Use IE's Shell Integration   198

How to Use IE's Active Desktop   200

How to Configure Internet
Explorer 4.0   202

Browsing Offline with Internet
Explorer   204

How to E-Mail with Internet
Explorer 4.0   206

How to Access Newsgroups with
IE4   208

How to Post to Newsgroups Using
IE4   210

How to Use Other IE4 Features   212

A Look at WebTV®   214

How to Download and Install
CU-SeeMe   216

How to Use CU-SeeMe   218

How to Download and Install Voice
E-Mail   220

How to Use Voice E-Mail   222

Index   224

INTRODUCTION

INK SPILLS on the Internet daily. It seems like each magazine I read contains an article on its usage, or some new technology to increase its usage, or news about the people that are using the usage. For instance, as I write this, I see seven articles on the Internet or Internet technology in the morning paper.

There is good reason for the hoopla. The Internet is an ocean of information and entertainment. There is something for absolutely everyone. That isn't a threadbare cliché, but a truth evident to anyone who has logged on.

Millions of people surf the Web, research FTP sites, or blast pixelated aliens on the Internet each day. For example, during the first week of NASA's Pathfinder mission on Mars, NASA site recorded over 3.5 million visits (commonly known as *hits*). That's just *one* of *millions* of Web sites. It seems like everyone is speeding down the information superhighway.

But they're not.

There is a significant number of people—smart people, computer owners—who have never heard the crackle, pop, screech of a modem's handshake. I'm not sure why, but I do have a theory, and I call it technophobia, and when Webster's decides to add it to their dictionary the definition will read:

Technophobia—n. the fear of technology, usually accompanied by animated gestures and the denial of use for said technology.

I know, I've been there myself. But, as I say elsewhere, "It's not rocket science." Your modem, computer, and Internet service provider (ISP) do all the hard stuff; you just have to click a couple of buttons. I'm here to teach you the right buttons to click.

I had a blast writing this book. I thought I was "Net smart" before I started—after all, that's why I applied for the job. But after a few months, hundreds of hours online, and a couple dozen application downloads later, I discovered just how much I didn't know.

I'd like to share my discoveries with you. So come on, if you're a technophobiac, face those fears. Turn the page, start reading, hook up, log on, and immerse yourself in the Internet ocean. Don't worry about drowning; you're holding the lifeboat in your hands.

Mark H. Walker
mwalker@neocomm.net

How t
You
L

PART 1

Understanding the Internet

DESPITE ITS SIZE AND DIVERSITY, understanding the Internet doesn't take a degree in rocket science. The influx of "normal" citizenry into what was once considered the realm of scientists and academics has broadened the appeal and accessibility of the Net. Black-and-green screen bulletin board systems have been replaced by sound and video–enhanced Web sites that you can browse with "point and click" tools.

In this part you'll learn what the Internet and its subset, the World Wide Web, are and what they aren't. Then we'll briefly look at Web addresses, explain e-mail, and browse a newsgroup or two. By the time you're done, you'll be ready to dive into Part 2 and *get online.*

IN THIS SECTION YOU'LL LEARN

- What Is the Internet?   2
- How the Internet Works   4
- What Is the World Wide Web?   6
- How the World Wide Web Works   8
- How to Read URLs   10
- What Is E-Mail?   12
- What Are Newsgroups?   14

What Is the Internet?

The Internet is a global collection of interconnected computer networks. The easiest way to understand it is first by examining small-scale networks, and then building, step by step, to a picture of the entire Internet.

1 A *network* is simply a bunch of computers that are connected (via cables, phone lines, high-speed data lines, or satellite) in order to share resources and information.

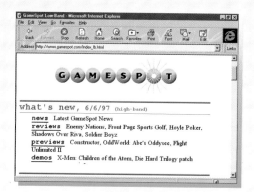

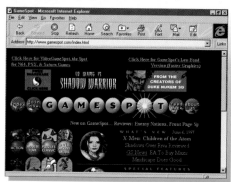

● No single entity controls the Internet. Rather, individual components are managed by various public and private institutions. Many Internet old-timers are deeply committed to a decentralized Internet—a slightly anarchistic place that welcomes the free exchange of ideas.

● Private networks aren't automatically hooked up to the Internet; they must connect, which requires special hardware and software, as described in Part 2.

● The Internet is much more than the sum of its parts; it also encompasses the incredible wealth of resources that are stored on Internet computers, as well as the contributions of millions of people who maintain and add to those resources.

7 In the "old days," it was hard to view anything but text-based documents on the Internet. That changed with the advent of the World Wide Web, because Web documents can include colors, graphic images, sound and video clips, animation, and more. Here are text-based and graphical views of Gamespot, a popular computer entertainment news site.

2 The term *local area network* (*LAN*) describes interconnected computers—all fairly close to one another physically—that not only share such hardware resources as printers but also software and data. A small company may have its computers connected in one LAN; large companies may have a separate LAN for each department and may then cable the LANs together to form a larger LAN.

3 In many LANs, there is at least one computer (normally a very fast one with a lot of disk space) designated as the *file server*. The other computers on the network can electronically access both programs and data stored on the file server, allowing people to share files without having to distribute them in printed form or on floppy disks. LANs also let people send e-mail to other people on the network and perform many other collaborative tasks.

4 Large businesses and organizations use high-speed data lines to connect LANs in separate geographical locations so that the staff in all their offices can communicate and share resources. This type of setup is called a *wide area network* (*WAN*). By using satellites or fiber-optic cables, WANs can even connect offices located on different continents.

5 The Internet is a motley yet effective assortment of large-scale WANs run by private companies (mostly long-distance phone companies such as AT&T, Sprint, and MCI). This backbone connects numerous private, commercial, government, and academic networks, as well as a growing number of home computers.

6 In its early years (the 1970s and 1980s), the Internet was used primarily by academics, scientists, and military personnel as a way of sharing work-related information and collaborating on projects. But scientists soon started using the Internet to share favorite recipes and gossip, and news of this new form of communication quickly spread to nontechnical people and companies around the world.

How the Internet Works

One of the reasons the Internet works is that all types of computers—UNIX-based machines, PCs, Macs, and so on—can connect and share information. This is possible because there are technical standards that dictate how computers on the Internet communicate with each other.

1 All computers on the Internet use a protocol called *TCP/IP* (*Transmission Control Protocol/Internet Protocol*). A protocol is a set of rules that delineates how computers communicate.

FYI

● TCP/IP allows multiple computers to share the same connection. Even if you have a very fast modem, heavy traffic on the Internet may cause slow access times, since the available bandwidth has to be divvied up among many users—kind of like asphalt and the rush-hour commute.

● In some areas of the country, you can connect your home computer to the Internet using the same type of cable that's used for cable TV. This type of connection is faster than either phone lines or ISDN.

7 The speed at which you can send and receive information depends on both the speed of your modem (or network connection in the case of a LAN) and the available bandwidth. *Bandwidth* is the capacity of data lines to carry Internet traffic.

Cheyenne Federal Savings Teddybear Savers Club

Official Membership

be it officially known that:

RANDY LEE KRAUS

is a certified member in good standing of the **Cheyenne Federal Savings Teddybear Savers Club**, and is hereby conferred with all rights and priviliges attributed thereto.

Be it hereby resolved that as a member of the **Teddybear Savers Club** I will reach my goal so that my Teddybear can "Hibernate."

Officially Authorized Signature

Cheyenne Federal Savings Teddybear Savers Club

Official Membership

be it officially known that:

LARRY BRENT KRAUS

is a certified member in good standing of the **Cheyenne Federal Savings Teddybear Savers Club,** and is hereby conferred with all rights and priviliges attributed thereto.

Be it hereby resolved that as a member of the **Teddybear Savers Club** I will reach my goal so that my Teddybear can "Hibernate."

Officially Authorized Signature

2 When you send a message across the Internet to another user, TCP divides the data into manageable units called *packets* and attaches to each packet the information necessary to reassemble the data and check for errors. IP then labels all the packets with a header containing the address of the destination and sends them on their way. During the trip, specialized computers called *routers* work to direct the packets along the most efficient paths. (In fact, separate packets may travel on different paths toward the same destination.)

3 Once the packets reach their destination, the computer on the receiving end removes the IP header and uses the data that TCP attached to each packet to make sure none of the packets have been lost or damaged. The packets are then reassembled into the original message. If the computer discovers a damaged packet, it sends a message to the sending computer asking it to resend the packet.

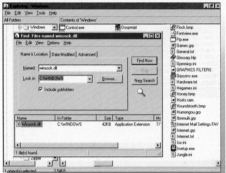

4 Computers need specific software to use TCP/IP. This software, often called the *TCP/IP stack*, is included in Windows 95. The visually prominent part of the TCP/IP stack is the WinSock shared library, or Winsock.dll, which is stored in your Windows folder. Because the TCP/IP stack is included in Windows 95, it's simple to connect a Windows 95 computer to the Internet (more about this in Part 2).

6 If you browse the Internet from a computer at work, you are probably connecting through a company LAN with an Internet gateway. A *gateway* is a special computer (often a router) on a LAN that communicates with the Internet at large. Where necessary, gateways translate between the protocol used internally on the LAN and TCP/IP, the protocol of the Internet.

5 The hardware used to connect computers to the Internet varies. If you access the Internet from home, you most likely use a *modem*. (Modems let the computer send and receive information over the phone line.) Some people use a faster type of access called *ISDN*. (See Part 2 for more about the hardware required to access the Internet from home.)

What Is the World Wide Web?

The World Wide Web is a vast collection of documents stored on Internet computers. Two things make Web documents (usually called Web *pages*) special. First, they contain *links* (either pictures or words you click on) that lead to other Web pages. Second, they contain graphics, sound, and so on, which open up new possibilities for presenting information. The Web is technically only one part of the Internet, but it has become so popular that many new Internet users believe the Web *is* the Internet.

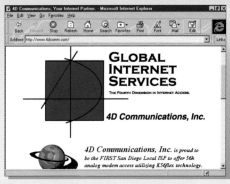

1 Computers that store Web pages are called Web *servers*. There is nothing special about these computers, except that they have a full-time connection to the Internet and they run Web server software. You access pages on Web servers by using a program called a *browser*. As soon as you tell your browser what Web page you want to view, it goes to the Web server that holds the page and retrieves it for you. Here is Microsoft Internet Explorer, a widely used browser.

● The relationship between browsers and Web servers is called a *client/server* relationship. The client (in this case your browser) requests information from the server (in this case the Web server containing the requested Web page), and the server delivers it.

● A Web server can support one Web site or many different sites. A Web site can also be so large that several computers are needed to handle all the requests from browsers.

● Since there is a risk that information you enter in online forms, such as your credit card number or your travel plans, could be intercepted by a "cyberthief," security is an important issue in interactive Web sites. For this reason, many companies are now developing secure Web sites that use cryptography to ensure that sensitive information isn't stolen. See Part 6 for the details about security on the Web.

7 Even though some Web sites have lots of bells and whistles, there is nothing wrong with simple text and graphic Web pages. One of the best things about Web pages is that they are easy to create and inexpensive to publish.

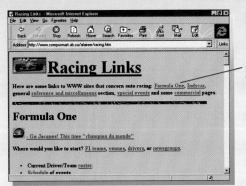

Links to other
Web sites.

3 The term *Web site* refers to a collection of one or more Web pages created by one person, company, or organization on the Web. At its simplest, a Web site can consist of just one page, but the Web sites of major companies normally contain dozens, or even hundreds, of individual Web pages, all linked together.

2 The links contained in Web pages can point to areas within the same page, to other pages residing on the same Web server, or to pages sitting on a computer on the other side of the world.

4 Web pages can also contain links to resources on the Internet that predate the Web, such as FTP and gopher sites. This makes the Web an ideal jumping off point for exploring the Internet, because it gives you access to all the things the Internet has to offer.

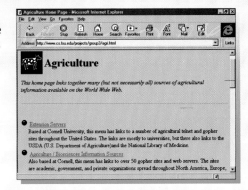

5 Web pages are becoming increasingly interactive. For example, instead of merely presenting information or graphics for you to view, many sites also include online forms to fill in and return to the site owner. These forms are useful for letting customers order products or fill in questionnaires. This example is a simple registration form for the Strategic Simulations Incorporated mailing list.

6 Web sites have grown quite sophisticated. As you'll soon discover, many Web sites include sound, animation, and video.

How the World Wide Web Works

A distinctive aspect of the World Wide Web is its linked pages; you can bounce from one page to the next by clicking special text or image links in the document. The ability to travel links is, for the most part, a good thing: You can easily explore related subjects, and you'll sometimes stumble onto real treasures you wouldn't have found otherwise. But you can run into trouble if you don't stay focused: Ten minutes into a concerted search for information about an upcoming ballot measure, you may discover that you're studying a page of tips for making a dynamite cup of coffee. Here's a look at what's happening behind the links.

Hypertext

Trendwatch

News from around and about the Web brought to you by Norman Dyer. He gives tips on shareware and trends with his assistant Hal to answer your most troubling questions.

1 The "clickable" text indicating links on a Web page is called *hypertext*. It is usually underlined and displayed in a different color than the surrounding text; when you point to it with the mouse, your mouse pointer typically takes on the shape of a pointing hand. Clicking on a hypertext link refers your browser to the document or sound file or video clip to which the hypertext is linked.

5 Companies with Web sites usually maintain their own Web server, and there are also companies that maintain Web servers for other companies.

● Increasingly, companies are using an additional protocol called *SSL (Secure Sockets Layer)* on their servers. This protocol encrypts data exchanged between the user and the Web site and keeps it secure. You'll learn more about secure sites in Part 6.

● The idea of hypertext has been around for a long time. For example, online help systems in many application programs use hypertext to allow users to quickly jump from one part of the help system to another.

2 The Web uses a protocol called *HTTP* (*Hypertext Transfer Protocol*) to transfer documents containing hypertext. HTTP's job is similar to that of TCP/IP: Both protocols tell computers how to communicate with one another.

3 You create Web documents using a markup language called *HTML* (*Hypertext Markup Language*). HTML is a set of codes used to format Web pages and create links. To a browser, the HTML code is like an instruction sheet telling it how to display the page.

4 Web pages reside on Web servers. A Web server is normally a fast computer with a lot of disk space that is running special server software. Most people who maintain Web sites from home rent space for their Web pages on a Web server managed by an Internet service provider (ISP). This makes your pages available continuously without the expense of keeping your own computer on-line 24 hours a day. (You'll learn more about ISPs in Part 2.)

How to Read URLs

To use the Internet efficiently, you need to understand URLs (uniform resource locators). Think of the URL as an address. Like an address it is comprised of several parts. Each part further specifies what you're searching for, until you arrive at the specific site, be it a Web page, sound file, or graphic image.

Protocol

1 The protocol is the first section of the URL. Typical options are http: (for Web sites), ftp: (for FTP or File Transfer Protocol sites), gopher: (for gopher sites), telnet: (for telnet sites), or news: (for newsgroups).

● Fortunately, you need not type the entire URL to find a location. Usually entering just the protocol and server name will take you to the site's home page. Once there, you can use the site's "in-house" links to navigate.

● Businesses on the Web *want* you to find their page. Frequently, you won't need to search, let alone type in a complete URL, to uncover a prominent page. For example, the address of the online version of USA Today is just what you would think—http://www.usatoday.com. So, often typing in http://www. followed by the company's name and .com will pull up the page you seek.

Anchor name

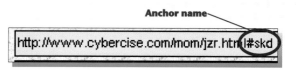

5 The last part of the URL is the *anchor name*. This section is separated from the rest of the URL by the number (#) symbol, and points to a specific section of a lengthy Web page.

Web server name

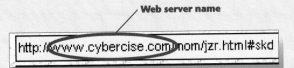

2 To the right of the protocol is the name of the Web server. This section of the URL normally ends with a forward slash (/).

Path

3 The next part points to a specific site within the server. This section starts and ends with forward slashes, and additional forward slashes are used to separate different parts of the path.

Back Forward Stop Refresh Home Search Favorites

Address http://www.usatoday.com/

Sports: Jazz bounce back with style in Game 3

BIG SPORTS WEEKEND

Inside
Nationline
Scores

USA TODAY

6/7/97 - Updated 1:29 AM ET

News
Sports
Money
Life
Weather

Document name

4 The fourth part of the URL is the name of the document. Web page file names end with .htm or .html.

What Is E-Mail ?

E-mail is an efficient business tool. E-mail is a great social aid. For many people e-mail is the single most important feature the Internet and online services offer. Whether memorandums distributed on the office LAN, book manuscripts sent across the world, or a short note to your best friend, e-mail is revolutionizing written communications. Here's a basic look at what an e-mail message is.

1 Just like its cousin "snail" or postal mail, e-mail has both a sending and return address in addition to the message. An address consists of the user's name followed by the @ symbol and the "location" of his or her mailbox.

Top-level domain

vfa146xo@nimitz.navy.mil

5 The last part of the address is the *top-level domain.* If the e-mail address is located in the United Sates, the top-level domain will be one of six: com (commercial organization), edu (educational institution), gov (government), net (networking organization), mil (military), or org (nonprofit organization).

FYI

● Foreign e-mail addresses use the country name abbreviation in place of or in addition to the top-level domain. Examples are de (Germany), uk (United Kingdom), and ca (Canada).

● E-mail addresses are not case sensitive and don't contain any spaces—despite what your AOL address may look like.

User's name

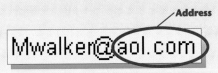

2 The user's name is usually some combination of his or her name, but this is not a rule. Although you can adopt any name that strikes your fancy, if you are doing business on the Internet, it's better to have a recognizable Net name.

Address

Mwalker@aol.com

3 The section after the name is the address. This frequently looks like a spilt bowl of alphabet soup, but it is straightforward in theory.

4 The first part of the address is the *host*. This is the computer that serves the account. The part immediately to the host's right is the *domain*.

Host — Domain

What Are Newsgroups?

If you were an amateur racecar driver, you might belong to the Sports Car Club of America (SCCA). Each month (when you weren't racing) you would get together with some other members and shoot the breeze about who won the latest race and how, discuss the current technology, or just spend time with like-minded friends.

That, in essence, is the idea behind newsgroups. They are places where like-minded folks can meet to exchange ideas on topics of common interest. Newsgroups are not real-time interaction. In other words, you won't engage in a phone-like conversation, but rather you post or reply to messages on subjects relating to the central topic of the newsgroup.

1 There are scads of newsgroups organized into major topical hierarchies: Comp (computers), sci (science), and misc (miscellaneous) are but a few. Obviously, within these hierarchies there are branches and subbranches.

4 Politeness counts. Without body language or voice inflections to aid your message, it's easy to be misunderstood. Go the extra mile to ensure your statement is not taken out of context—a simple *<g>*, which means grinning, can take the bite out of most any sentence.

● Newsgroups are a great, albeit occasionally risky, place to market used computer games, cars, refrigerators—just about anything. Be careful, however. If the person you are dealing with is not willing to provide their phone number, drop the sale (or purchase) like a hot potato.

● You can print a particularly interesting *post*—or newsgroup message—by selecting the message, then clicking on the print icon in whatever newsreader you are using. You can also save messages to file; see Part 7 for details.

2 You can find groups that interest you with Deja News, a newsgroup search engine, which you will learn more about in Part 4.

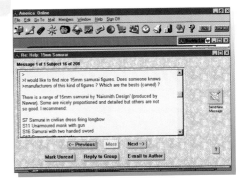

3 You may post and read messages with any *newsreader*. AOL has a good one, as does either of the browsers from Microsoft or Netscape.

P A R T 2

Hooking Up

"IF A TREE FELL IN THE WOODS with no one to hear, would it make a sound?" The Internet is similar to the lonesome tree of that well-worn brain teaser. The vast resources of the World Wide Web, FTP sites, and gopher sites would be for naught if people could not browse, download, and research them.

Simply put, the Internet will do nothing for you until you use it. And to use it you must hook up and log on.

Don't worry if you are unsure what to do—you've come to the right place to find out. These pages explain the hardware and software you need to get up and running. First we'll describe the hardware and then discuss selecting an Internet service provider, or ISP. Next we'll walk you through installing and configuring two of the most popular browsers: Netscape Navigator and Internet Explorer. There is also a segment on connecting to on-line services, such as America Online, CompuServe, and the Microsoft Network.

The final section covers the nuts and bolts of dialing in and explains to overcome some of the problems you may face. Certainly there is more to using the Internet than included here (that's why this book has seven more parts); however, once you read "Hooking Up," you'll be able to log on and start breathing your bit of life into the Internet. At least if something falls you'll be around to hear it.

IN THIS SECTION YOU'LL LEARN

- **The Hardware You Need to Access the Internet**   18
- **How Your Modem Works**   20
- **How to Choose a Local Internet Service Provider**   22
- **How to Install Netscape Navigator**   24
- **How to Configure Navigator**   26
- **How to Install Internet Explorer**   28
- **How to Configure Internet Explorer**   30
- **Installing Online Services**   32
- **How to Dial In**   34

The Hardware You Need to Access the Internet

Although the number of people participating in the Internet grows daily, many more—frightened by the alleged complexity of the system—stay away. A friend of mine put off connecting for months because he didn't know how to install a modem, he said. Finally committed to signing on, he took his computer to a local service store and asked the technician to install a modem.

"Can't," the technician said.

"And why not?" replied my indignant friend.

"You already have one installed."

Just as with my friend, many of our worst tech-fears are imagined. As I said in the beginning of the book...it ain't rocket science.

1 The first thing you need is phone service. Yes, there are other ways to hook up, but the jack in your wall is the easiest. Those who are frequently online should get a second phone line for the modem—to reduce marital tension.

8 Modems are normally not difficult to install. Remove your computer's cover, plug in the modem to the motherboard, button up the computer, and run the supplied software. If you have Windows 95, it often detects the new hardware and mates the applicable driver with it.

● If you bought a computer within the last year, chances are the modem is installed already. Spin the computer around and look at the back. If there are phone jacks, it probably has a modem. Of course checking in the **Device Manager** tab under the **System's Properties** in the Windows 95 **Control Panel** will provide the same information.

● Although modem setup is frequently a snap, it can be frustrating. An improperly installed modem can conflict with other hardware and drivers, making you, and your computer, miserable. Perhaps the easiest way to install a modem is to take your computer to a qualified technician. Let them fight the installation wars.

7 ISDN requires a special phone line, which your phone company will provide, and either an internal card, called a terminal adapter, or an external ISDN modem (a misnomer, since it is no longer modulating analog data to digital), both of which you can purchase from a well-equipped computer store.

2 You'll also need some phone cable (the type that connects your phone to the wall) and a splitter, unless you have a dedicated modem line. Both are available at small technology shops and in the electronics section of larger department stores.

3 Of course, you need a computer. Minimum specifications would be a 486/100 Mhz with 16MB of memory (RAM) and about 25MB of free hard disk space (for browsing software). The faster your system—as measured in MB of RAM, generation (Pentium vs. 486), and Mhz—the better off you'll be.

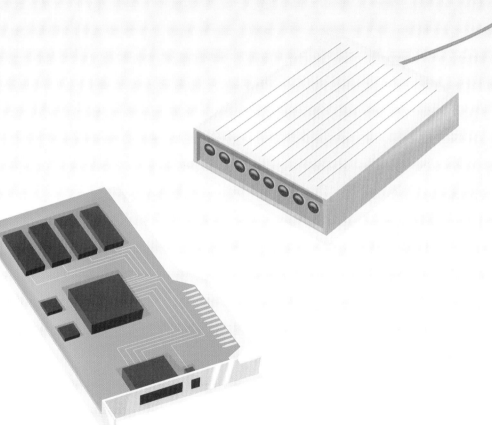

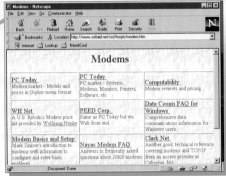

4 And you need a modem. These come in two breeds: the ubiquitous internal and nearly extinct external. Internal modems mate to the motherboard inside your computer. External modems, which look like smallish eight-track tape players or largish portable CD-ROM players (depending on your generation), plug into the back of your computer and require an external power source.

6 A costly, yet quicker, option is *ISDN* (Integrated Services Digital Network). ISDN phones transmit data in digital, instead of analog, format and can race up to 128 kbps. This service is usually available from your phone company.

5 28.8 kbps (kilobits per second) is pretty much the standard speed. Anything less is just too slow. There is much hoopla over the coming 56 kbps-capable modems and the phone lines that can handle them. Although they appear to be the technology of the future, a 28.8-kbps or 33.6-kbps modem is fine for now.

How Your Modem Works

Modems, and data transmission, are the black arts of the computer industry. Hyper-regulated, with committees on committees deciding exactly what the standards will be, it's hard to get through the gobbledygook and find out what you need to know.

The good news is, you don't need to know much to understand, in layman terms, how a modem works. Follow along and I'll explain the basics.

1 The word *modem* is derived from the term *MOdulator-DEModulator*. Similar to a radio, a modem takes a signal, changes its properties, and transmits it; then another like system receives it on the other end.

● If this brief discussion has piqued your interest, point your browser to one of the numerous sites on the Web that provide technical explanations of modem functions.

● Which modem you buy depends on what you want to do. If you plan on spending hours browsing the Web, playing games, and downloading files, buy the fastest setup your wallet can support. On the other hand, if you are merely exchanging e-mail with a couple of friends, you can limp by with a 14.4-kbps modem.

● You may buy a 56-kbps modem, and your ISP may say they support 56-kbps modems, but how fast you connect depends more on the phone lines on your street than anything else. Before investing in this cutting-edge technology, talk with others in your area who own them. What is their connect speed? Talk with the phone company. Do their lines support the new modems? Buy only if you are sure you can use the faster speed.

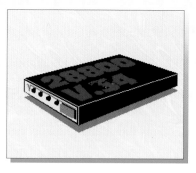

5 The host modem receives and translates your information into a digital form the host computer can use. The host, in turn, will process any data request generated by your transmission, perform the function, translate the results into analog data, and return the information to your computer.

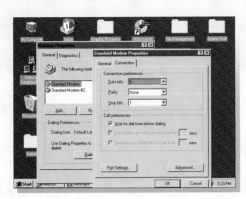

2 Before you send information, your modem needs to connect with the receiving modem. There are several settings in your modem's protocol that must be set in order to do this. Fortunately, Windows 95 or either of the Netscape products will set these for you. In the old days (three years ago) you had to manually set these parameters (Stop, Bits, Parity) to connect with the receiving modem. If you *must* adjust these settings, they reside in the Control Panel, Modem, Properties, Connection tab.

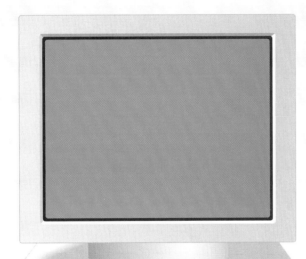

3 Once properly connected to the receiving, or host, computer, your modem is ready to send data. To send the information from your computer to another, the modem changes the information from its digital form to analog data.

4 The speed at which a modem can transfer data is rated in kilobits per second, or kbps. As we said earlier, 28.8-kbps modems are the norm. Anything less than 14.4 kbps is worthless, and the new 56-kbps technology, while promising, is still a little rough around the edges, at least when used with an analog phone line.

How to Choose a Local Internet Service Provider

The World Wide Web has been called the Gold Rush of the 1990s. If that's true, then Internet service providers (ISPs) are the general stores selling picks and shovels. There are many important factors to consider when choosing your ISP; cost, ease of access, customer service, and reliability are but a few. Fortunately, with the incredible popularity of the Web, there are a large number of ISPs to choose from. If you do some careful shopping, you'll be able to find an ISP that meets your needs perfectly. In this section, you'll learn what to look for and what to avoid when deciding on an ISP.

NEOCOM supports triple standard (X2, K56Flex & ISDN) in Martinsville/Henry County.

1 Make sure your prospective ISP offers what you need. To access the Web, you need either a SLIP (Serial Line Internet Protocol) or PPP (Point-to-Point Protocol) connection. These special types of connections are different than a simple dial-up Internet connection. Make sure your ISP knows that you require access to the World Wide Web.

● You may want to inquire about the ISP's own connection to the Internet. Since the Net is a network of networks, your ISP needs a fast connection to the Internet to provide the best service. Ask your ISP for a diagram or explanation of how they connect to other networks and at what speeds.

● Finding an ISP can be as easy as looking in the yellow pages. If none are listed, ask a salesperson in a computer store or talk to anyone you know who is a computer buff. If you can't get a specific recommendation about an ISP, you can probably learn how to contact the local computer user society where information and opinions about ISPs are plentiful. Last, but certainly not least, check out your local chamber of commerce business listing.

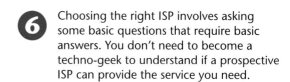

6 Choosing the right ISP involves asking some basic questions that require basic answers. You don't need to become a techno-geek to understand if a prospective ISP can provide the service you need.

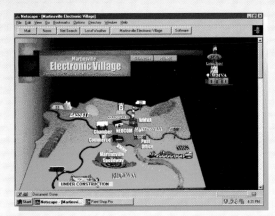

3 Access speed is important. Make sure your ISP supports high-speed modems. Even if you have a fast 28.8-kbps modem, it won't help if your ISP only handles 14.4 kbps.

2 Another key factor is locality. To eliminate long-distance phone calls, your ISP should be based in your local calling area. On the other hand, you may choose a commercial online service or larger nationwide ISP, both of which provide local dial-in numbers.

4 Service and support are important. Your ISP should be willing to make it easy for you to get online, walking you through the setup if necessary. Your ISP should also provide free and immediate technical support, 24 hours a day.

Small business page on local server

5 If you plan on creating your own home page, ask your prospective ISP if they offer space for Web pages. Keep in mind, however, that you don't need to use the same ISP for both dial-up access and Web page hosting. You can shop around for the best rates for each type of service.

How to Install Netscape Navigator

N etscape Navigator was one of the first Web browsers, and it's still one of the most popular. It combines a point and click interface with a sophisticated yet easily understandable browsing engine, and it has pulled many Web surfers into the Netscape camp.

For those of you who choose not to install an online service, Navigator, available for download from the Netscape Web site or distributed directly from many ISPs, will make an excellent browser and e-mail tool.

1 If you have disks, pop them into the applicable drive. In Windows 95 select Start and then Run, and browse your drive until you locate the install program. It will usually be a program that ends with .EXE. Double-click on the program, and you are off to the races.

● **Simply closing the Netscape program window doesn't disconnect you from your ISP. To break the phone connection, you need to click the Disconnect button in the Connected message box. If you want your ISP connection to automatically disconnect after a specified length of time with no activity, right-click on the icon for your connection in the Dial-Up Networking folder, click on Properties, click on Configure, click on the Connection tab, mark the check box Disconnect a Call If Idle for More Than 30 Mins, change the number of minutes if desired, and then click on OK twice.**

● **Check Netscape's home page (http://home.netscape.com) frequently. Navigator and Microsoft are constantly improving their browsers. It's a good idea to keep yours current.**

Dial-up icon

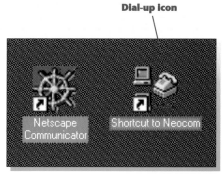

6 Once the installation is complete, you'll have (at least) a Dial-up icon that connects you with your server and a Navigator icon that launches the browser. Now you're ready to double-click the Dial-up icon and sign on.

2 If you have downloaded Navigator, be sure to save it to your desktop (so that it's easy to find). Double-click on the downloaded file's icon to start the setup.

3 Navigator will prompt you to enter the installation directory. The default is normally C:\Program Files\Netscape. I prefer C:\Netscape because if, for some reason, you need to find the directory, it is more likely to jump at you if it is not layered inside another directory.

4 Netscape Navigator software obtained from local ISPs or bought at the store includes an Account Setup Wizard that walks you through configuring your modem to connect with the ISP.

5 A little care will go a long way as you complete the installation. Make sure you enter your password and ISP phone number correctly.

How to Configure Navigator

Installing Navigator is only half the battle. The other half is adjusting the software to meet your needs and your system's requirements. Navigator is a versatile tool. It allows you to configure your e-mail's appearance, what security precautions you take, what applications start when the browser boots, even the home page it initially displays.

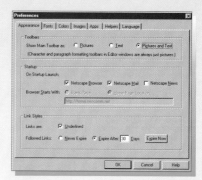

1 Use the general preferences, located under the Options menu, to set the Netscape applications your browser starts and how it displays the main toolbar. If the toolbar is set to display text rather than pictures, your browser will be slightly faster.

● You can also alter the way your bookmarks are organized. We'll cover this in greater detail in Part 3 because if your bookmarks aren't organized, they serve little purpose. After all, you bookmark sites so you can *easily* return to them. Make it a habit to routinely organize your bookmarks by category.

● Passwords are curious beasts. The password you need to protect your ISP account, and hence your access to the Internet, is serious business. Treat it as such. Don't be cute: Make it indecipherable, mix capital with lowercase letters and numbers. On the other hand, this makes the password tough to remember. Here's a trick I've learned: Create a sentence, such as "I have a 7 year old daughter," and use the initials—Iha7yod—as your password. It works great and is nearly unbreakable.

6 You can also configure the way the screen appears. Hiding the toolbar or address window, for example, provides more "viewable" area on your monitor.

2 Make your favorite Web site your startup page. In the Options menu, click on General, followed by Appearance. In the Startup section, type the name of the page you want to start with in the Browser Starts With box, then click OK and you're done.

3 It's also important to check your mail and newsgroup settings. Without the correct addresses here, you won't be able to send or receive mail. This information is supplied by your ISP. If you are unsure about what to enter in the boxes, call their technical support.

4 Network preferences allow you to decide how your computer will deal with the Internet. Most of this is fairly technical; however, Netscape does provide an excellent, tab-specific, online help routine. If you are unsure of what these terms mean, they are best left alone.

5 You can set a password under security preferences. This will keep others from using your browser while you're away. To do so, click the Password tab and then the Password button, and follow the instructions.

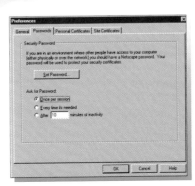

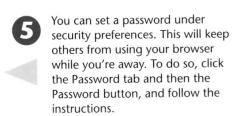

How to Install Internet Explorer

In 1995 Microsoft released Internet Explorer, and the browser wars were on. For the first time Netscape had a legitimate competitor for top dog in the browsing arena. Although there are critics of each, both are quality products that provide most of the tools you need to stay afloat while surfing the Web.

These pages cover downloading and installing Internet Explorer. Alternatively, you may purchase a copy of Microsoft Plus, which includes Internet Explorer (in addition to numerous beautiful screen savers and other options).

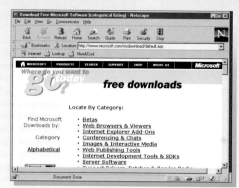

1 To download Internet Explorer, direct your browser to the Microsoft download site located at http://www.microsoft.com/msdownload/default.asp. This is an index page where you choose the Microsoft product you wish to download.

● As we said, IE initially takes you to the Microsoft registration page. While you are in the Microsoft Web page complex, it is a good time to browse and download any interesting plug-ins. Chat 2.0 is a standout. The program, formerly titled Comic Chat, splashes a cartoon character on the monitor to assume your personality while you type. Perfect to break the monotony of a long business day.

● If you are downloading a new version of Internet Explorer, I—not Microsoft—recommend uninstalling your previous version first. The older IE will ask if you want to keep your history folders. Click Yes and your previous addresses and bookmarks will be saved and subsequently imported into the new version of IE.

5 Once you have signed on, IE will pull up the Microsoft registration page. Fill it in and add any plug-ins or add-ons you wish, and you are ready to browse.

2 Again, for convenience, save the download to your desktop. Once you have the file safely stored on your computer's hard drive, double-click on the applicable icon (usually something like msie302m95.exe) on your desktop.

Click here to move up through your folders.

3 If you are unsure how to download to your desktop, follow these instructions: After the Save As dialog box is displayed, click on the little yellow up-arrow folder icon until you reach the screen that displays your desktop. This window will show a miniaturized representation of the icons and folders on your full-sized desktop screen. Saving to this directory will place an icon for the saved file on your desktop, where it can be easily found.

4 After asking the typical questions about directories and such, Explorer will install. Once it's installed, an Explorer icon will appear on your desktop. Double-clicking on it will start the Microsoft Account Setup Wizard. If you already have an ISP account, use its existing data.

How to Configure Internet Explorer

Microsoft Internet Explorer has matured into a full-fledged Web browser, capable of giving Netscape a run for its money. Internet Explorer 3.02 incorporates most standard audio and video formats and ActiveX controls. The following pages demonstrate the basics for configuring and browsing with Internet Explorer.

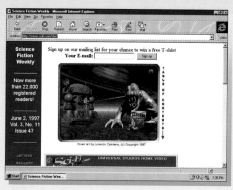

 Internet Explorer has a simple toolbar for Web navigation and access to basic functions, such as printing and searching. The arrow buttons allow you to browse through Web pages you've previously visited in the current session. The font control buttons adjust the size of the default font for the bi-focalled among us.

● Internet Explorer supports context-sensitive menus. If you right-click your mouse in the browser window, you'll have quick access to special features.

● Internet Explorer now offers you the ability to control the content accessible through the browser by enabling industry standard Internet ratings. You can filter out Web sites with mature ratings or no ratings at all.

● Internet Explorer also supports a VRML (Virtual Reality Modeling Language) with a special plug-in. This allows you to browse VRML sites, which are simulated 3-D worlds. You can use the keyboard arrows or drag your mouse cursor to walk around in a VRML world. A toolbar at the bottom of the VRML window provides additional navigation options, as does the pop-up menu accessed by right-clicking anywhere in a VRML world.

6 To read Usenet newsgroups, you must have an Internet provider that operates a newsgroup server running the NNTP news protocol. To access the newsgroups, choose Read News from the Go menu.

2 You can store your most frequently visited Web sites in the Internet Explorer Favorites list. To add the current site to your list of Favorites, click the Favorites button on the toolbar or choose Add to Favorites from the Favorites menu.

3 You can edit and maintain your Favorites list by choosing Organize Favorites from the Favorites menu. Each URL in your Favorites list is a shortcut. You can add, edit, and delete your shortcuts, and even create subfolders to organize them. The Favorites folder works just like a Windows 95 Explorer window and supports drag and drop and right-click menus.

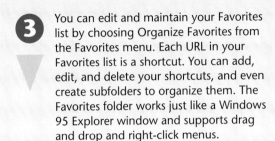

4 You don't have to limit your URL shortcuts to the Favorites folder. Because Internet Explorer is tightly integrated with Windows 95, you can place your URL shortcuts almost anywhere, including on the Windows 95 desktop. You can drag a shortcut into the Internet Explorer window to go immediately to that site. If Internet Explorer isn't running, you can double-click on any URL shortcut to launch Internet Explorer and navigate directly to that site.

5 Internet Explorer 3.02 comes with its own e-mail software built in. To use Internet Mail, click the Mail and News button on the toolbar. Keep in mind that to use Internet Mail you must first configure it by selecting Mail from the toolbar, then Options from the drop-down menu, and filling in the appropriate information.

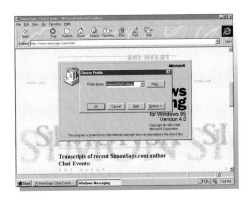

Installing Online Services

Web traffic has increased rapidly through commercial online services. America Online (AOL), CompuServe, and the Microsoft Network (MSN) have all opened their doors to the Internet and now provide extensive access to the World Wide Web.

Getting up and running on the Web via one of the commercial online services is typically easy, especially for novices. Although the Web browsers that the online services provide aren't as sophisticated as Netscape Navigator or Internet Explorer, they're certainly adequate for basic Web surfing.

The best part about browsing the Web via an online service is that very little setup is required. If you're already a member of AOL or CompuServe, you'll be surfing the Web in a matter of minutes. If you're a member of MSN, you already are.

● **AOL offers free versions of their software that you can use for a trial period to explore their offerings and determine whether you wish to become a subscriber. AOL will mail you a complete software package, along with installation instructions. Call 1-800-827-3338 to receive the free trial software.**

● **If you're having trouble with the AOL Web browser, or if you just want to find out more about it, explore the Internet Connection area on AOL. The Internet Connection has numerous files, help documents, and question-and-answer forums dedicated to helping AOL users surf the Web. Click on the Internet Connection button in the AOL Main Menu or use the keyword *Internet*.**

● **When browsing with MSN, if you click the Reveal Toolbar icon, you may find that the toolbar disappears again as you move through the MSN choices. Just click again to bring it back.**

1 Setting up one of the online services is as easy as, if not easier than installing Navigator or Explorer. Each walks you through with nearly fail-safe instructions.

8 The latest version of Microsoft Network provides plenty of powerful features to help you get the most out of your trip on the World Wide Web. The robust support for animation and sound enhances your experience.

7 As with AOL, if you like a site, you can bookmark it by clicking the heart with the little plus sign in its lower-left corner. Choosing the adjacent heart displays a list of your favorite places.

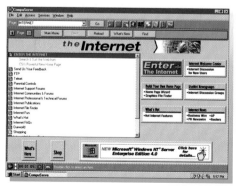
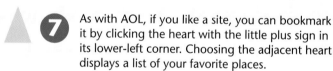

6 To begin browsing the Web while logged on to CompuServe, select the Internet button from the main menu, then click on Enter the Internet. Once on the Internet screen, you can enter a URL in the "page" address block or use the inverted arrow to the right of the URL address block to call up the last sites visited.

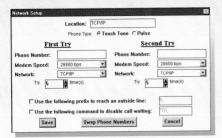

2 Both the Microsoft Network and CompuServe will configure their systems to work with your existing Internet connection during setup, but AOL will not. To use your local ISP to access AOL, you will have to click on the Setup button from the Welcome screen. In the Setup menu, select Create. Type **TCP/IP** in the Location box, leave the Phone Number box blank, set your modem speed, select TCP/IP as the network, and you are ready to do business.

3 All three online services require a screen name and password. Once these are entered, you may save them. On one hand, saving them minimizes the time it takes to log on, but on the other, it allows anyone with access to your computer to access your Internet accounts. For your home computer this is not necessarily a bad thing. For the office, however, it is probably best *not* to save your password. I mean, why go to all the trouble to think up a cool password, then save it so it is never required?

Click this button to bookmark a site.

Click here to view your bookmarks.

5 Selecting the inverted triangle to the right of the URL address box will pop up a list of sites visited during the current session. Double-clicking on a site will return you to that location.

4 AOL's Web browser contains the basic tools you need to cruise the information highway. AOL allows you to bookmark favorite sites by clicking on the small heart on the screen's top-right corner. Selecting the folder with a heart displays your bookmarks, both for AOL and the Internet.

How to Dial In

Honestly, if you've read this far, you have probably logged on. Many of us, however, who have installed the browsing software or on-line services are somewhat unsure of what to do when it comes to finally hooking up.

This topic briefly explains how to get those data packets flowing through your phone line. Follow along, and you'll be browsing with the best of them in no time at all.

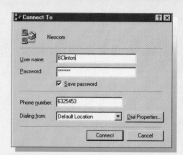

1 Clicking on the Internet Explorer, Netscape Navigator, or MSN icon will display the connection box to your ISP.

● If you access your browser, whether it's an on-line service browser or other browser, through your ISP, you can run as many browsers as your computer's RAM permits. To do so, minimize your current browser and start another. This comes in handy if you need to check your mail on separate accounts or wish to chat with a friend on AOL while you browse with Netscape.

● Determine if your ISP has alternate access numbers. If so, make a dial-up connection for each. To do so, click on the Dial-up Networking icon in the Control Panel, select Make New Connection, and fill in the boxes presented.

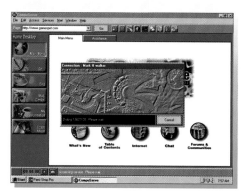

5 On the other hand, if you are using the CompuServe, AOL, or MSN proprietary numbers, just double-click on the on-line service's icon and...presto! Just 45 seconds and two busy signals later, you're online—just kidding about the busy signals.

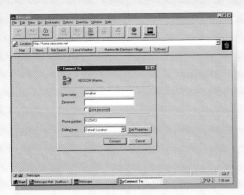

2 If you have not already saved your password, you will need to type it in and click Connect. This will dial up your ISP and establish a connection.

3 Once you are connected, your browser will display your selected home page. (If you are running Navigator and have chosen to start mail on startup, your mail application will run, notifying you of any new messages on your server.)

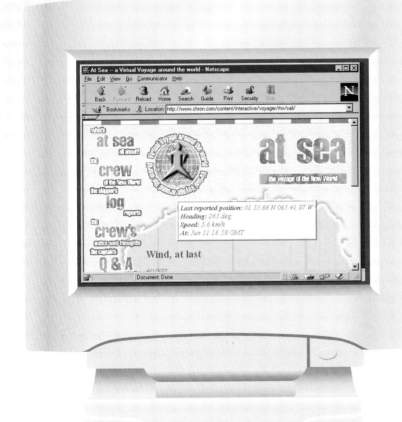

4 If you are running AOL or CompuServe through an ISP, you must first connect to the ISP (utilizing the Dial-up Networking Connect To window), then click on the AOL or CompuServe icon. It's a tad more cumbersome, but no big deal.

How t
Your

L et'
y
of

Using the Browser

ONE DAY, browsing the Web will be as commonplace as scanning the yellow pages, and navigating cyberspace will be as simple as driving to the corner store. However, we're not there yet, so a few pointers on negotiating the Web will help your browsing go more smoothly. As we wait for data-transfer technology to catch up to the demands of the Web's content, learning the quickest way to get from point A to point B will keep thumb-twiddling to a minimum.

This section begins with a lesson on the basics of displaying new Web pages. Then you get a grab bag of useful techniques for moving back and forth among Web pages you've already visited, and you'll learn how to mark Web pages for quick retrieval and how to organize your pages according to topic. And since sooner or later you'll visit a page divided into multiple sections, or *frames*, we'll explain what frames are and what to expect when you maneuver in them.

Then we'll take a look at some of the Web's multimedia technologies: listening to sound, viewing movies, and using your computer as a telephone.

IN THIS SECTION YOU'LL LEARN

- How to Display Web Pages — 38
- How to Navigate among Web Pages — 40
- How to Navigate Frames on a Page — 42
- How to Use Netscape Navigator Bookmarks — 44
- How to Set an Internet Explorer Favorite — 46
- How to Update Your Favorites and Bookmarks Automatically — 48
- How to Listen to the Web with RealAudio — 50
- How to Watch Web Movies with QuickTime — 52
- How to Use the Internet as a Phone — 54

How to Display Web Pages

There are two basic ways to tell your browser what page to retrieve. You can enter the URL for the page, or you can click a hypertext link (or a specific part of an image) that leads to the page. Also, if you visit one page frequently, you can instruct Netscape Navigator or Microsoft Internet Explorer to display that page automatically on startup. The steps shown here assume you've already started your browser—Navigator, for instance. If you haven't, start the program and connect to your ISP.

1 If you know the URL for a page, you can enter it directly in the Location text box near the top of the Navigator, or Internet Explorer, window. Just click anywhere in the text box to select the current URL.

7 To change Internet Explorer's startup page click on View, then Options, followed by the Navigation tab. Type in the home page address you wish to use and click OK.

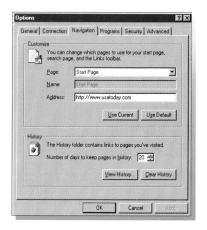

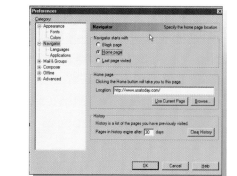

6 By default, the Navigator browser displays Netscape's own Web site when you first launch the program or when you click on the Home button in the toolbar. (If you don't see the toolbar, choose View, Show Toolbar.) To change this default Web site, choose Edit, Preferences, and, if necessary, click on the Navigator from the file skeleton. Then enter the URL for the site you want to see at startup and click OK.

● When using Navigator, instead of typing the URL directly into the Location text box, you can enter it in the Open Page dialog box. To display this dialog box, press Ctrl+L—this method is just a bit quicker.

● You can search for text in a Web page with the Find command. Click on the Find button in the Navigator toolbar (the same command is in the Edit menu in Internet Explorer) to display the Find dialog box, type the word you're looking for, and click on the Find Next button. Navigator highlights the first instance of the word. This technique is useful when you're looking for specific content in a long Web page.

2 Type the URL for the desired page. As you type, your text replaces the previous URL and the label for the Location text box changes to Go To. Press Enter to retrieve the page. (If you click a second time on the existing URL before typing, you can edit the URL rather than replace it.)

3 Both Netscape Navigator and Internet Explorer display the status of the transfer in the bar at the bottom of the window.

Status bar

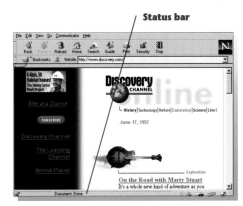

4 Once the transfer is complete, the status bar displays "Document: Done." The transfer can take a couple of seconds, several minutes, or more, depending on the speed of your modem, other network traffic, the location of the server holding the page, and the complexity of the page.

5 Clicking on hypertext links is another way to navigate to a site. When you point to a link, the mouse pointer usually becomes a hand (in most browsers), and the URL of the page that will be retrieved appears in the status bar. Note that some links are embedded in graphic images. An image that contains links is known as an *image map*.

URL of hypertext link

How to Navigate among Web Pages

On the previous page, you learned how to travel to new areas of the Web. Here, you'll learn how to get back to places you've been, without retyping URLs. These navigation methods are nice when you've accidentally followed links down the wrong road and want to retrace your steps, and they can cut down your time online.

1 In every browser we've seen, you can return to the previous page by clicking on the Back button on the toolbar. If you are viewing a previously visited page, you can return to the most recent page by clicking the Forward button.

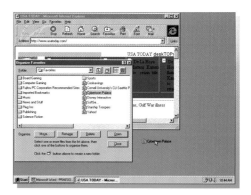

7 If you're using Internet Explorer, you can create a shortcut by clicking on Favorites, then selecting Organize Favorites, and then dragging a page's icon to the desktop.

● If you select a URL in the Location text box and then double-click on the Chain Link button, Navigator copies the URL to the Windows Clipboard. You can then paste the URL into any other application program or into an e-mail message.

● You can also create a shortcut to a Web page by right-clicking on a page to display a context menu and then choosing Internet Shortcut. In the Create Internet Shortcut dialog box that appears, edit the description or the URL if you choose, then click on OK.

● Clicking on Internet Explorer's Address bar will display a number of Microsoft's picks for hot Web pages, including Best of the Web and Web Gallery.

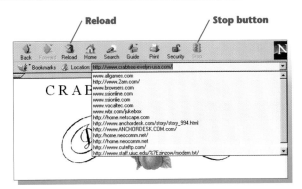

Reload   Stop button

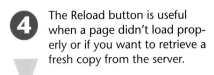

3 If you entered a URL or clicked on a link, and it's taking an intolerably long time to retrieve the page, you can stop the transfer by clicking on the Stop button on the toolbar.

2 Netscape Navigator keeps track of the last 15 URLs typed in the Location text box. If you want to return to one of these locations, click on the drop-down arrow at the right of the text box to view the list of URLs, and click on the one you want.

4 The Reload button is useful when a page didn't load properly or if you want to retrieve a fresh copy from the server.

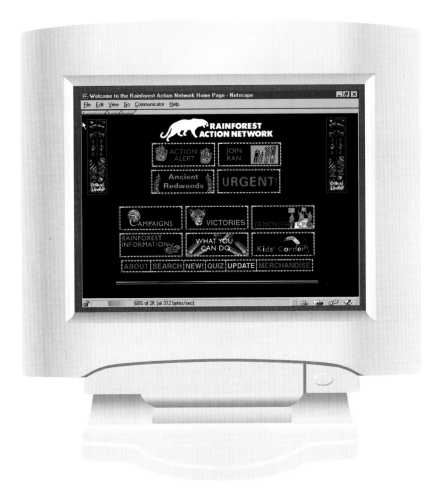

Chain Link button

5 The Chain Link button is to the left of the Location text box in Navigator. You can use this button to create a shortcut icon on the Windows desktop for a particular Web page. First, display the page in question, and then, if necessary, click on the Restore button in the upper-right corner of the Navigator window so that some of the desktop is visible.

6 Next, drag the Chain Link button onto the desktop. Your mouse pointer changes into a small square containing a curved arrow. Drop the link and you have a new shortcut to the page.

How to Navigate Frames on a Page

As you wander the Web, you'll find many sites that use frames. *Frames* are independent, scrollable panes within a Web page. They are useful for two reasons: First, they let the Web designer place information in a window that stays visible regardless of where the user has scrolled in the page. Second, the contents of multiple frames can be interlinked, so that clicking on a link in one frame retrieves the linked information into a separate frame.

1 The Web site shown here, for Montana's Flathead Valley (http://www.fcva.org/flathead), is divided into three separate frames.

● Frames are somewhat graphic intensive (as is Java programming). If your computer and modem combo are not up to the strain, check to see if the site offers a "low-end graphic" version. Usually this will eliminate frames (and Java scripting).

● Frames are created using standard HTML code. To learn about frame programming, check out *How to Use HTML 3.2* from Ziff-Davis Press.

2 The frame at the top is a *ledge*—a frame that always stays visible and stationary as you navigate in the frames underneath. Companies frequently use ledges to display their name and logo.

3 Like many sites that employ frames, this one uses a frame on the left to list the main categories of information at the site. When you click on a category, such as Communities, related information is displayed in the frame to the right, below the ledge.

4 You can further manipulate the contents of the right-hand frame by clicking on the subcategories in the area just above it (Bigfork, Columbia Falls, and so on).

How to Use Netscape Navigator Bookmarks

The Web is nonlinear. You may randomly follow a dozen links before reaching a page that tickles your fancy. So, when you find a page you want to visit again, Navigator lets you bookmark it. Then you don't have to worry about writing down its URL or memorizing the trail of links that got you there.

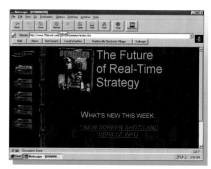

1 When you land on a page you'd like to bookmark, issue the Bookmarks, Add Bookmark command (or press Ctrl+D). This adds the bookmark to the bottom of the Bookmarks menu. To use the bookmark later, simply display the Bookmarks menu and click on the bookmark.

8 Once you've reorganized your bookmarks, open the Bookmarks menu again. You will see the new folders you created, and when you point to each one you will display the submenu listing the individual bookmarks.

● Typically, you'll add bookmarks to the Bookmarks menu as you are browsing, and then periodically go into the Bookmarks window to drag the new bookmarks into appropriate folders.

● You can add a new bookmark and place it in its correct folder in one step. To do this, display the Bookmarks window, and resize both it and the Netscape window so that the two windows are displayed side by side. When you want to bookmark a page, drag the Chain Link button (to the left of the Location text box) over to the desired folder in the Bookmarks window.

● To delete a bookmark, click on the bookmark in the Bookmarks window and press the Delete key.

Drag bookmark to folder.

7 In the Bookmarks window, to move a bookmark into a new folder, drag the bookmark from its current location to the folder and release the mouse when the folder name is highlighted. Continue creating folders and moving bookmarks into them until you've brought order to the chaos. When you're done, click on the close button (the X) in the upper-right corner of the Bookmarks window to return to the Netscape window.

2 As you can imagine, the list of bookmarks in the Bookmarks menu can quickly become too long to be of much use. To organize your bookmarks in a logical fashion and simultaneously shorten the list in the Bookmarks menu, you can create bookmark folders (or even folders within folders). Netscape places folder names near the top of the Bookmarks menu with black triangles to their right. When you point to a folder name, a submenu appears with the bookmarks in that folder.

Bookmark folder ———

Bookmark ———

3 Before you start organizing your bookmarks, you should familiarize yourself with the Bookmarks window. Start by choosing Bookmarks from the Window menu (or pressing Ctrl+B). This displays the Bookmarks window.

4 In this example, there are already folders in the window, They are shown with small plus or minus signs. Clicking on a plus sign displays the bookmarks in a folder; clicking the minus sign hides them.

6 In the Bookmark Properties dialog box, type a name for the folder and optionally enter a description. Then click on OK.

5 To create a new folder, select Go to Bookmarks from the Bookmarks dropdown menu. Next, select Item from this menu and then select Insert Folder.

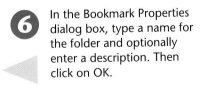

How to Set an Internet Explorer Favorite

F avorites are Internet Explorer bookmarks. Their use is identical to Navigator bookmarks; saving and organizing them is nearly identical, and the interface is similar. Nevertheless, there are enough differences to warrant a brief explanation.

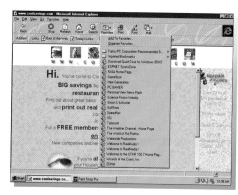

1 To create a Favorite, click the Favorites button and select Add to Favorites from the drop-down list.

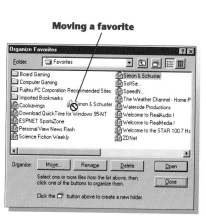

Moving a favorite

5 Organize your favorites by dragging and dropping them in the folder of your choice. The favorite will disappear from the Organize Favorites window; click the file's new home folder to locate it.

● Clicking on the List icon (the top-right icon in the Organize Favorites dialog box) will display data on the files in the box. The data includes the type of file, when it was created, and its size.

● As previously mentioned, you can drag a favorite from the Favorites window to your desktop, creating a shortcut. Clicking on this shortcut icon will boot Internet Explorer, open your Dial-up box, and take you to the Web page.

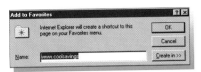

2 Internet Explorer will offer a name for the favorite. However, you can name it yourself by typing over Microsoft's offering and then tapping Enter.

3 Pull down the Favorites menu and click on Organize Favorites to create folders and arrange your favorites.

Click to create new folder.

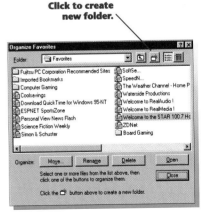

4 You can create a new folder by clicking on the folder with a burst. Type the folder's name and hit Enter.

How to Update Your Favorites and Bookmarks Automatically

There's a lot of information on the Internet. To be honest, there's a glut of information on the Internet—and it's growing each day. Whether for business or pleasure, you have probably set aside several sites that contain information you want to keep current on.

Unfortunately, it takes time to check your favorite sites. Several companies, however, have developed software that will not only automatically update your information but add new sites to your list of "must see" pages. Additionally, most of these add-on applications will, through the use of caching, allow you to view sites off-line.

FYI

● Netcaster is not the only software available that automatically updates your bookmarks and allows you to browse off-line. Webwhacker from ForeFront (www.ffg.com/internet.hmtl) and Surfbot 3.0 (ww.specter.com) are two others. Both incorporate many of the same features as Netcaster.

● On startup, Netcaster is set to update sites automatically once a day. You can change this, however, to whatever suits your fancy—weekly, hourly, anything.

1 Netscape's Netcaster is a top-notch off-line browser. The software, which is compatible only with Netscape Communicator 4.0, makes keeping "Web-fluent" a snap.

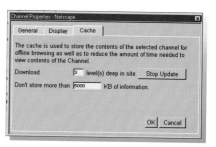

5 To add a channel click Add in the left of the Netcaster toolbar. The Channel Properties dialog box will appear. Fill in the appropriate boxes and click OK. (The number of levels you direct Netcaster to download represent how deeply the program will delve into a site. The first level is the site's home page, the second is the next page in the site, and so on.)

2 You must download Netcaster separately from Communicator. Netcaster will install automatically. To launch it, click on Netcaster in the Communicator pull-down menu. Be advised, it takes a while (3-7 minutes) for Netcaster to initially load.

3 To view a site off-line, move the cursor over the channel's (that is, the Web site's) address. Underneath the name, a mini-menu appears. Click the Update button.

4 To browse a site off-line once Netcaster has downloaded the site, start Communicator, then Netcaster. Once Netcaster is running, click the site's address in My Channels.

How to Listen to the Web with RealAudio

The Web talks, no kidding. But, unless you put your ears on, you'll never hear it. The most famous set of ears available is RealAudio 3.0 from Progressive Networks. Once plugged in, this free application beams radio stations, sports events, and a host of other sound waves through your computer. Here's how to download and install this amazing software.

1 Ensure you have a 16-bit sound card, such as Sound Blaster. The Progressive Networks software will not work without it.

7 Alternatively, if you own a 28.8-kbps modem, you can purchase and download RealPlayer Plus. RealPlayer Plus offers improved sound and image quality, a scanning routine, and buttons—similar to those on your car radio—to lock in your favorite "Real" stations.

6 Now, you'll be able to listen and watch real time audio and video from the Web. Be sure to check the RealAudio page frequently for updates.

● There is no need to create a path from RealAudio to each of your browsers. The RealPlayer and RealAudio installation routine checks for installed browsers and loads the proper drivers to service them.

● Progressive Networks offers a list of recommended sites on their home page. Click on the RealAudio showcase and demos under the More RealAudio and Video heading.

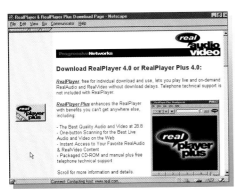

2 Call up the RealAudio home page. It is located at **http://www.realaudio.com/.** Once you arrive, choose your download.

3 RealAudio 3.0 transmits sound in near real time (there is some buffering). Because of this, RealAudio requires at least a 14.4-kbps modem.

4 RealPlayer (which includes both RealVideo and RealAudio) broadcasts both video and audio clips in near real time. There is a catch: RealPlayer requires a 28.8-kbps modem to work.

5 Download to your desktop and double click the downloaded file. The Progressive Networks Install Wizard will guide you through the installation.

How to Watch Web Movies with QuickTime

QuickTime is an application, originally developed for Macintosh computers, that displays digital movies, including sound, text, and graphics. QuickTime is a *cross-platform* application; in other words, the software works on Macs and PCs and plays several different file types (.MOV, .MPEG, and .AVI).

Unlike RealPlayer, you must download a QuickTime movie before you view it. You can view the portion of a file that has downloaded so far; however, the movie will come to an abrupt stop when the data ends.

- Digigami offers a QuickTime enhancement (available at www.quicktime.apple.com) titled Movie Screamer. Screamer helps bridge the gap between QuickTime and RealPlayer. When using Screamer, as with *progressive download* technology, you can view the movie as it is downloaded.

- There is lots of neat stuff you can do with QuickTime movies—embedding them in your Word documents, for instance. To do so, pull down the Word Insert menu and select Object. Under the Create New tab, select QuickTime movie. Next browse until you find the movie you wish to insert, then click Open, and save your document.

- Microsoft's ActiveMovie also plays most multimedia files. ActiveMovie's progressive download technology plays the file while it is still downloading. You can download ActiveMovie from the Microsoft download site at www.microsoft.com/msdownload/default.asp/.

- Numerous sites have a large collection of videos. One of the best is NASA's gallery of space movies. You can access it from NASA's home page at http://www.nasa.gov/.

1 To download QuickTime 2.1.2 (3.0 is coming soon) cruise to the QuickTime home page at **http://quicktime.apple.com**. Scroll to the "Latest QuickTime Releases" header, and select your platform. Save the file to your desktop.

6 To save the file to disk, right-click on the image and choose Save. The Save Movie File dialog box appears; select the file's destination and save it.

5 Right-clicking on the movie image will pop up a list of advanced options. Depending on the type of file playing, you may resize, loop, save, or edit the image display.

2 As always, double-click on the file to install it. During install, QuickTime will, if you have more than one browser on your computer, ask you which one you wish to install QuickTime for. Select your preference and move on. If you wish to install for more than one browser, you'll have to install QuickTime again.

Clicking with 'hot' cursor plays QuickTime file.

3 To play a QuickTime file, click on the file icon or hypertext link. You will have to wait while the file is buffered into your computer's memory. A status bar on the bottom of the view screen displays the percentage of the file that has loaded.

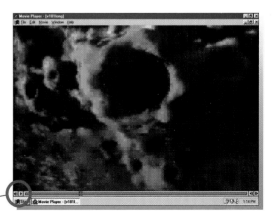

QuickTime control buttons

4 When the file has finished loading, you can click on the VCR-type play button to view the file. Clicking the stop button will stop it. The speaker button on the far left changes the movies volume.

How to Use the Internet as a Phone

Would you like to chat with your sister across the country, but you can't afford the phone bill? Worry not, the Internet has an answer. Perhaps the most interesting Web technology to emerge in recent years is *Internet telephony*.

Internet telephony enables you to talk, albeit at a reduced voice quality, with anyone who has similar software and a TCP/IP Internet connection.

1 FreeTel is a free Internet telephony application. To download the software, head to **www.freetel.com**.

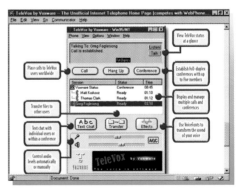

7 There are many more Internet telephony applications available on the Internet, such as TeleVox by Voxware (www.voxware.com). Additionally, Netscape offers one of its own, Cool Talk, available at **http://home.netscape.com/comprod /products/navigator/version_3.0 /communication/cooltalk/index.html**.

● If you like, you can send text instead of voice transmissions. When using FreeTel, to toggle the voice/keyboard option, click the Keyb button.

● You can also send data (that is, a file) while talking. In FreeTel click the Send menu, then type in the name of the file you wish to send. Alternatively, you can "browse" until you locate the file.

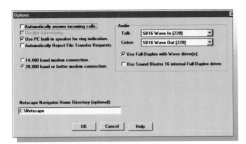

2 Download and install FreeTel. Pay close attention to the warning on Sound Blaster 16 Duplex. Since it disables the sound for other Windows applications, you should think twice before using it.

3 Connect, via your ISP to the Internet, and double-click on the FreeTel icon.

4 The large window in the center of the FreeTel window is the Electronic Phone Directory. Double-clicking on any name in the box will "dial" that person. Once connected, you can talk, using your computer's microphone, and listen through its speakers.

5 To accept an incoming call click on the Accept button. This will only work when someone is trying to call you.

6 If the person you're calling is already talking with another party, the "busy" message will appear.

How t...
Your...

PART 4
Searching the Web

THE AMOUNT OF INFORMATION available on the Internet, and specifically, the World Wide Web, brings to mind an old saying: "Be careful what you wish for—you may just get it."

The Internet holds data on every imaginable topic, from computer games to Constantinople. Unfortunately, finding it is not always easy. That's where we come in. The following pages will get you started on your Internet exploration.

Once you've discovered how to find the big stuff—Babylon 5's home page for instance—we'll show you more advanced searching techniques. Using these techniques will find exactly what you want, without your having to browse hundreds of return "hits."

After reading these pages, you'll be able to find information on anything you desire—even if it is who's playing computer games in Constantinople while they watch Babylon 5.

IN THIS SECTION YOU'LL LEARN

- Web Search Engines 58
- How to Find Search Tools and Navigation Aids 60
- How to Use Yahoo! 62
- How to Use Lycos 64
- How to Use InfoSeek 66
- How to Use AltaVista 68
- How to Use Excite 70
- How to Use AOLNetFind 72
- How to Use HotBot 74

Web Search Engines

The number and, to some extent, complexity of Internet search engines is daunting. Search engines will hunt through the millions of Web pages or search the billions of postings in the Newsgroups. This topic provides a brief overview of them.

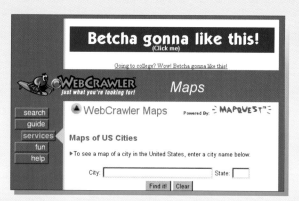

1 Many search engines clamor for your browsing attention. Some, such as WebCrawler, are best for searching Web sites. Others are better for searching through news-group postings.

4 You'll learn how to employ search routines to avoid returns like the one above.

● Searching the Web is more an art than a science. If there is one rule of thumb, however, it would be this: The more specific your search, the better your results.

● There are plenty of search engines available, but try to pick a favorite and stick with it. The more familiar you are with the application, the better the results you will get.

2 Some will even automate your search. Informing you of new information posted on the Web.

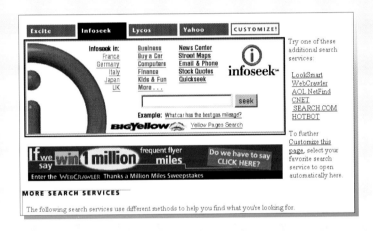

3 Despite the variety of search engines, search *routines* are similar. Most, if not all, use the same language to delineate and modify your query. For instance, *Boolean operators*—like AND, OR, and NOT—allow you to search for documents that contain exactly your desired words or phrase. These operators must appear in ALL CAPS and have a space on either side in order to work. Some search engines have a shorthand notation for these operators: pluses for AND, minuses for NOT, for instance. We'll show you more such examples as we explore the various search engines.

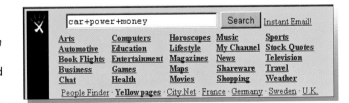

How to Find Search Tools and Navigation Aids

Once you have found one navigation aid on the Web, chances are you have found them all, or at least all the well-known ones. All of the most popular navigation resources have sections with hyperlinks to the other prominent resources.

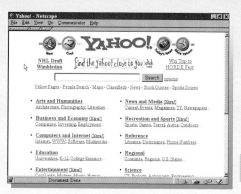

1 The first comprehensive directory for the World Wide Web was Yahoo!. Although it sounds like the holler of a happy cowboy, this resource ranch has made quite a name for itself out on the wild Web frontier. In the next topic, you'll get the details on how to use Yahoo!. If you'd like to take a quick peek now, saddle up your Web browser and mosey on over to **http://www.yahoo.com**.

● In some cases, these resources will list more than just Web sites. The hierarchical databases will often have sections for FTP sites, Usenet newsgroups, gopher sites, and more.

● Some search engines have resources that point to "cool sites" or "sites of the week." Since these sites are specifically picked by people who review hundreds of sites each day, they are usually worth a look.

● Obviously, these are not the only search applications we'll examine; however, these engines are an example of what is available.

4 You can access the home page of the AltaVista search engine by navigating to **http://www.altavista.digital.com/**.

2 The Web is big enough for more than one directory, especially if the people that created Lycos have anything to say about it. Lycos will be covered in more detail later. Like Yahoo!, this resource is worth a quick look right now. Plug the following URL into your browser: **http://www.lycos.com**.

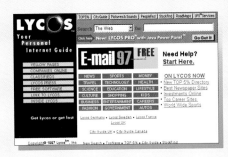

MORE SEARCH SERVICES

The following search services use different methods to help you find what you're looking for. Check them out.

SEARCH ENGINES	WEB GUIDES	WHITE & YELLOW PAGES	TOPIC SPECIFIC	TIPS
AltaVista	Excite	Bigfoot	100hot Web Sites	
AOL NetFind	Infoseek	Four11	AutoWeb Interactive	
Electric Library	LookSmart	GTE SuperPages	Health InfoNet	
HOTBOT	Lycos	ON'VILLAGE	Thomas Register	
WebCrawler	CNET SEARCH.COM	WhoWhere?	of American Mfrs.	
	Yahoo!	World Pages		

3 Another recommended navigation resource is InfoSeek. Check it out by pointing your browser to **http://www.infoseek.com**.

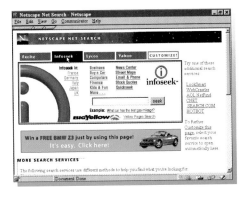

How to Use Yahoo!

Yahoo! is one of the most popular search tools on the Web. Like other navigation resources, it offers both the user-defined seek-and-retrieve style search and an extensive subject list indexed by category.

1 Start at the Yahoo! home page by entering the URL **http://www.yahoo.com** into your browser's location box.

8 Yahoo! returns a list of matches based on the information you supplied. If you click on any of the hyperlinks that Yahoo! provides, you'll be taken either to a new Web site or to a list of sites in the Yahoo! directory.

● For an excellent guide to Web sites for kids, move to the bottom of the Yahoo! home page and click the Yahooligans! For Kids link, or simply enter the URL http://www.yahooligans.com.

● Yahoo also provides a lengthy list of Web and Internet search resources. Follow the Yahoo directory path Computers and Internet: Internet: World Wide Web: Searching the Web.

7 Enter a word or words to search for in the search text box then click on the Search button. Yahoo! will take a few moments to process your request.

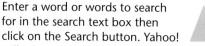

2 To navigate through the Yahoo! site using its basic hierarchical directory, first pick a topic, such as Computers and Internet. This will show you a list of lists that fall under the general heading. Click on a link that interests you.

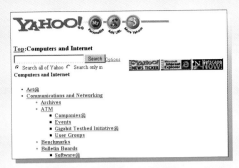

3 You will see a listing of subcategories under the Computers and Internet heading. As you continue to move from the general to the specific, you will see the path of your category search displayed at the top of the window. Follow the path of your choice to view the Web sites listed.

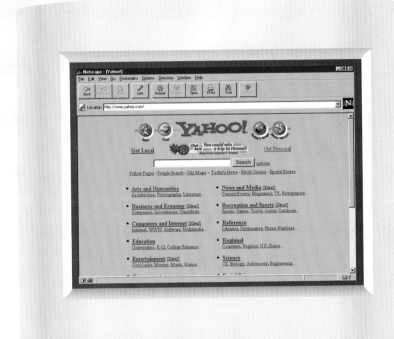

4 Return to the Yahoo! home page by clicking on the word *Yahoo!* at the top of the screen.

5 Now let's try the fill-in form search. You can type a keyword, such as *knitting*, in the text entry box, and Yahoo! will scour its database for matches. Click on the Options link to the right of the Search button for ways to narrow your search.

6 These search options help you control your search. If you enter more than one keyword, specify whether Yahoo should look for documents containing any of the keywords or only for documents that contain all of the keywords. Another setting allows you to stipulate the areas to be searched. You can also limit the number of matches Yahoo! returns at a time. The default setting is 20.

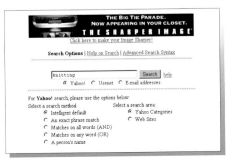

How to Use Lycos

Lycos combines a powerful search engine with a subject directory of sites, organized into 16 major categories. In addition to full-text search capability, Lycos offers the ability to conduct Web searches specifically for graphics and sounds.

1 Start at the Lycos home page. Point your browser to **http://www.lycos.com**.

- It is sometimes difficult to determine from a document title whether it contains the information you seek. To see a brief description of the article, select Standard Results or Detailed Results from the last option on the Custom Search page.

- For a comprehensive look at all the features available, check out the Lycos Site Map at http://www.lycos.com/sitemap.html.

5 In addition to the title of the document found, Lycos indicates the percentage of success and the number of search terms found in each article. This information is placed in parentheses at the end of each document title. However, a success rate of 100% does not always mean that all search criteria were found, but rather the closest match was found.

2 To perform a Lycos search, you enter some keywords and tap the Go Get It button. Try entering several words to see how Lycos interprets your request. For example, type the words **ancient Chinese artifacts** into the text box.

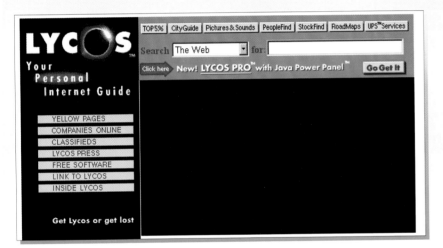

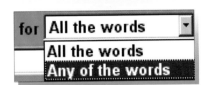

3 Customize your quest by choosing your search method—"all the words" or "any of the words." By matching any of the words, the probe will return documents containing any one or more of the three words in our ancient Chinese artifact search. After setting your options, click the Go Get It button to begin the search.

4 As you can see, Lycos returns several results that match the search criteria. Each of the documents selected contains at least one of the search words. Had you instructed Lycos to match all the words in the search options, only those documents containing all three search words would have appeared. (Note that even if more than one of the search words is present in the document, they are not necessarily together or in the same order in which you entered them in the search box.)

1-10 of 17756 relevant results
Just the links Standard Descriptions Detailed Descriptions

1) Paragon - Bronzes
PARAGON HOME PAGE TABLE OF CONTENTS GLOSSARY OF ABBREVIATIONS PLACE AN ORDER CHINESE BRONZES Vi...
http://webart.com/paragon [100%, 3 of 3 terms]

2) Sinorama Magazine - The national Museum
[Subscribe] [Sinorama Home Page] [GIO Home Page] [Comment] The national Museum: AWindow on Seve...
http://gio.gov.tw/info/si [89%, 3 of 3 terms]

3) HUMANITIES PROGRAM CONTRACTS
SAMPLE HUMANITIES CONTRACTS A student seeking a Humanites major develops, in conference with th...
http://www.dla.utexas.edu [36%, 2 of 3 terms]

4) http://www.h-net.msu.edu/~rhetor/threads/chinese.html
>>> Item number 529, dated 95/10/25 09:14:47 -- ALL Date: Wed, 25 Oct 1995 09:14:47 -0...
http://www.h-net.msu.edu/ [35%, 2 of 3 terms]

How to Use InfoSeek

The heart of InfoSeek is a powerful and comprehensive search engine coupled with one of the most extensive databases of Web pages on the Internet. InfoSeek was originally a subscriber-only service, but it is now supported solely by advertising, and, as such, is available free of charge.

1 Go to the InfoSeek home page at **http://www.infoseek.com**.

7 If certain words need to appear in the document but the specific order does not matter, preface them with a plus sign. For example, to search for documents that must contain the word *cheese* and may also contain the words *eggs* and *milk*, type **+cheese milk eggs** in the search text box.

6 To refine your search further, you can modify the keywords. For example, to search on an exact phrase, enclose your keywords in quotes. For example, if you type **cow jumped over the moon**, InfoSeek will return documents containing any of the five words. However, if you enclose the keyword phrase in quotes, InfoSeek will only return documents with all of those words in the exact order you entered them.

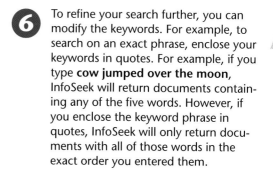

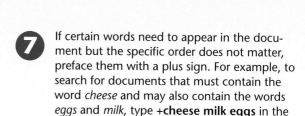

2 Enter keywords to search for in the text entry box. For example, to seek information on the best laser printers for the PC, type **laser printer pc best**.

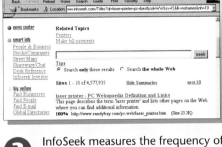

3 InfoSeek measures the frequency of the specified keywords in the documents of its database and sends results in groups of ten, sorted by relevance.

4 InfoSeek also maintains a directory called Topics to help you find a particular subject area. You can navigate through the Topic section and its subtopics, and then perform a search within that topic. On the other hand, it's easy to browse the topics until you find a page that tickles your fancy.

5 Use the Source drop-down list to limit your search.

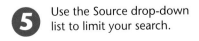

How to Use AltaVista

The AltaVista search engine is a free service from Digital Equipment Corporation, and it boasts one of the largest databases of Web pages available. It also features a flexible search query language, which makes it an ideal tool for Web power users.

1 Start at the AltaVista home page. Point your browser to **http://altavista.digital.com/**.

6 AltaVista's Advanced Query provides more sophisticated searching. Click the Advanced Query icon at the top of the page to access this feature. The Advanced Query gives you more control over your searches, and lets you determine how the search should weigh the results. Click the Help icon at the top of the page for complete instructions.

5 Constrain your keyword searches to certain parts of a Web page by typing a special prefix for the part of the page to search, followed by a colon and the keyword or phrase. For example, to search for the keyword spam, but only when it appears in the title of a Web page, type **title:spam** in the text entry box. The other specifically searchable parts of a Web page are the URL, the host, or a link contained anywhere in the page.

● **AltaVista's Surprise link (at the bottom of the page) will take you on a random jump to somewhere else on the Web. Click the Surprise icon and then select a category. You'll jump to one of the millions of Web pages in AltaVista's database.**

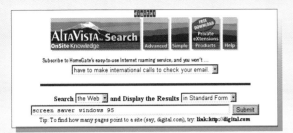

2 AltaVista supports two search types: simple and advanced. Most of the time you'll use the default simple search. First, enter the keywords for your search in the search text box. For example, to search the Web for information on screen savers for Windows 95, type **screen saver windows 95**.

3 A few moments later, the AltaVista search engine returns its results. As you'll notice, there are quite a few possibilities—perhaps more than 30,000 matches—because AltaVista is looking for documents that contain any of your keywords. You can refine the search using the plus sign to indicate required keywords and quotation marks to mark phrases. For example, to refine the previous search, type **+screen +saver +"Windows 95"**. This will return only documents with all three search terms found.

4 Using the drop-down selection boxes, you can perform your search on either Web documents or Usenet newsgroups. You can also choose your result display type, which can range from compact (single-line listings) to detailed.

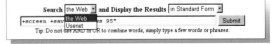

How to Use Excite

Excite (http://www.excite.com) includes both a directory of reviewed sites and a search engine. Excite's strong suit is its ability to search by concept, as well as exact keywords. If you type the keyword *airplane*, for example, Excite will also find Web pages about planes, jets, aircraft, and flying machines, mixed in with the occasional Jefferson Starship fan page.

1 Type your keywords in the search text box and click Search. Use a plus sign in front of a keyword to make sure that the word is contained in the search result, and use a minus sign to exclude Web pages containing the word.

6 You can check the Excite News section of Excite's home page to find the day's top news stories, and you can use the Excite Reference section to find directory services, free software, dictionaries, maps, and more.

● If you want to search newsgroup articles instead of Web sites, select Usenet Newsgroups in the Where drop-down list.

● Type keywords in lowercase if you want to find both lower- and uppercase instances of the word. Only use uppercase letters when you want to limit the search to the words that match the combination of lower- and uppercase you type.

2 By default, Excite sorts the Web pages it found by *confidence*, with the best matches at the top. To sort the results by site instead, click on the Sort by Site button (located at the top of the search results page).

3 Sorting by site shows you at a glance which Web pages in the results come from the same site. To go back to sorting by confidence, click on your browser's Back toolbar button.

4 Excite lets you use the operators *and*, *or*, and *not*. Connect two keywords with *and* if you want to find only Web pages that include both words (the same as prefacing the words with plus signs). Use *or* to find pages containing at least one of the keywords. Precede a keyword with *not* to exclude pages that contain the keyword (the same as prefacing the keyword with a minus sign). You can also use parentheses to group search criteria together.

5 To use Excite's directory of reviewed sites, click on one of the main categories in the Excite Reviews section of the Excite home page.

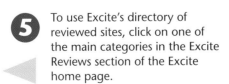

How to Use AOLNetFind

America Online's AOLNetFind is a powerful new search application that can not only be used while on AOL but accessed from other browsers also. Although similar to the search engines we discussed earlier, it is nevertheless worth a quick look.

1 AOLNetFind is located at **http://www.aol.com/search**.

7 AOLNetFind also includes a list of sites. Clicking on one will take you to a submenu with more specific choices. It's a nice way to browse areas that interest you.

6 AND NOT will exclude a word or phrase from the hunt. For example, *Ford AND NOT Henry* will call up a ton of hits for Ford trucks and cars but none on the man that founded the company.

● AolNetFind also has as list of recommended AOL and Internet sites. One of the best is NETFind Kids Only. Clicking this link will pull up a host of kid-related sites.

2 As with any other search engine, type the name of the concept, or exact words you are searching for, in the text box.

3 You can refine your search with Boolean operators—AND, OR, AND NOT—as well as quotation marks. To work, the operators must be capitalized and have a space before and after the word.

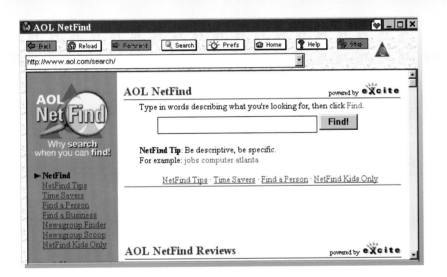

4 AND will locate documents that have both indicated keywords, in any order. Words grouped in quotation marks will bring up documents that have the words in the same order. For example, *"Joan Jett" AND music* would likely return pages on the venerable female rocker.

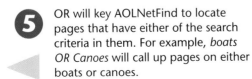

5 OR will key AOLNetFind to locate pages that have either of the search criteria in them. For example, *boats OR Canoes* will call up pages on either boats or canoes.

How to Use HotBot

The HotBot search engine and site list are promoted by HotWired—the same people that publish *Wired* magazine. Daily increasing in popularity, HotBot meshes the best traits of other search engines with a couple of new concepts, and has a user friendly format.

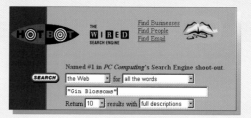

1 Go to the HotBot Web page, **http://www.hotbot.com**.

6 Use the tabs on the left side of the page to narrow your search further.

● You can save the parameters of previous searches and use them again. Click on Save This Search for more information.

● HotBot also has a layered information directory at the bottom of the page. Clicking on one of these categories will send you strolling down its information path.

2 Enter the topic you wish to hunt in HotBot's search text box.

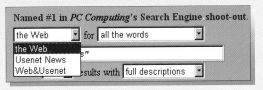

3 Choose where you wish to search by clicking the box to the right of the Search button.

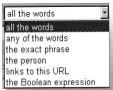

4 Click on the "for" box to modify how HotBot will use the words you've typed to retrieve documents. You can look for data that has all the words, any of the words, the exact phrase or several other options.

5 You can also specify whether you want returns as full descriptions, brief descriptions, or URLs only.

PART 5
Using the Internet

SURFING THE WEB is fun; there are a lot of neat sites to explore. The Web doesn't, however, scratch the surface of the Internet's potential. The Internet offers a multitude of interactive and semi-active pastimes—applications to download, cyberpeople to meet, and information to digest.

To fully realize these possibilities, however, we must learn to do more than browse through the latest Java-powered Web page machines. The Internet has many nuggets of information hidden in its dusty corners. To find them, we must learn how to use more than our browser.

IN THIS SECTION YOU'LL LEARN

- How to Save and Print a Web Page   78
- How to Download a Program   80
- How to Install Downloaded Files   82
- What Is FTP?   84
- How to Connect to an FTP Site   86
- How to Navigate in an FTP Site   88
- How to Download Files from an FTP Site   90
- How to Upload a File to an FTP Site   92
- What Is Telnet?   94
- How to Set Up Netscape Navigator to Use Telnet   96
- How to Connect to a Telnet Site   98
- How to Navigate in a Remote Application   100
- What Are Gopher Sites?   102
- Visiting a Gopher Site   104

How to Save and Print a Web Page

In your travels around the Web, you will occasionally come across information that you'd like to save to disk. Perhaps you visit a site frequently for certain reference data; opening a file from disk is usually much faster than connecting to a Web site. Or maybe you found a graphic that you'd like to use; to use such an image in your own document, you need to first save it to disk. Netscape Navigator lets you save entire Web pages in a couple of different formats; you can also save the graphic images from Web pages, or save just a portion of a Web page by doing a little cutting and pasting. Alternatively, you can print Web pages from your browser without saving them to disk.

1 When you want to save an entire Web page, display the page, then choose File, Save As to bring up the Save As dialog box.

8 To print a Web page, display the page in Navigator, click on the Print toolbar button (or choose File, Print) to bring up the Print dialog box, and click OK.

● If you save an HTML file from the Web and then open it in a word processing program, the document won't display as it does in a browser; instead, you will see all the actual HTML codes.

● If you right-click on a link, Netscape Navigator displays a context menu containing the Save Link As command. Choosing this command saves the linked page without retrieving it to the screen. (You can also do this by holding down the Shift key as you click on the link.)

● If you want to save the contents of a frame, click inside the frame once to make it active, and then choose File, Save Frame As. You can print the contents of an individual frame by clicking on it and choosing Print, Print Frame. (When a page containing frames is displayed, the Save As and Print commands become Save Frame As and Print Frame.)

7 If a Web page contains a graphic image you'd like to save, right-click anywhere on the image to display a context menu, and choose Save Image As to bring up the standard Save As dialog box. You won't need to choose a format for graphic files because Navigator automatically retains the original format— either .GIF or .JPG.

2 If you want to preserve the page formatting, leave HTML Files selected in the Save As Type drop-down list to have Navigator save the Web page with all of its HTML codes. You can later use any browser to view the file (in Navigator, choose File, Open File), which will appear as it did when you viewed it live through your browser. Note, however, that Navigator does not automatically save graphic images contained in Web pages. See step 7 to learn how to save graphics.

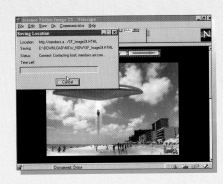

3 To save the Web page as plain text without any of its original formatting, choose the Plain Text option in the Save As Type list box.

4 After you've chosen a format in the Save As Type list box, enter a name for the file in the File Name text box, select a location for the file in the Save In list box at the top of the dialog box, and click Save.

5 The Saving Location message box appears briefly as Navigator saves the Web page.

6 If you want to save only a portion of the text in a Web page, highlight it first by dragging over it with the mouse. Then choose Edit, Copy to copy the selected text to the Windows Clipboard. Now you can paste your selection into a word processing document (select Edit, Paste).

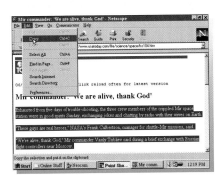

How to Download a Program

As you may know, programs are comprised of dozens, if not hundreds, of individual files. When software developers want to make a program available for downloading, they compress all the component files into one large file, which they often place on the Internet. *Downloading* is the process of copying this file onto your hard disk. On the next few pages, you'll learn how to download and install a trial version of a shareware plug-in named Starfish InternetMeter (http://www.starfishsoftware.com). This plug-in uses the Navigator window to display your session time, data transfer rates, and connection status.

1 Begin by reading any download instructions at the site. This information is usually located on the same page as the link that actually downloads the file. Many sites list the hardware and operating-system requirements for the programs you can download and provide brief explanations of how each program works. It's a good idea to read this information carefully to confirm that the software will run on your system and that it does what you want it to do.

7 When the file transfer is completed, Navigator closes the Saving Location dialog box and leaves you on the same Web page. You can now close your Internet connection, close Navigator, and turn to the next topic to learn how to install the software.

● If you download all your software from company-sponsored sites, you are less likely to get viruses. It's much safer, for example, to download a new version of Netscape Navigator from Netscape's Web site than from a site named Willy WebWizard's Home Page.

● If you get disconnected during a download, you must start over. In step 4, Navigator will ask you if you want to replace the existing file. Click Yes to download a new copy and overwrite the partially transferred file.

6 You can do other work on your computer during a transfer, but the download may take longer. Because the computer has to share its resources with the other programs you're using, it can't squeeze those kilobytes in as quickly.

2 Once you've decided to download a file, follow links until you get to the one that actually initiates the download. This link is frequently the word *download*, but it varies. Click on the download link, and then go to step 3 if you see the Unknown File Type dialog box, or to step 4 if you see the Save As dialog box. If you're downloading a file with the .ZIP extension and you have WinZip version 6.1 (or later) on your computer, the WinZip Wizard might (depending on your setup) automatically download the ZIP file, extract its component files, and install the software for you. If this happens, you should skip to step 5 on the next page, "How to Install Downloaded Files."

3 If the file you're downloading has an extension that Navigator doesn't recognize, it displays the Unknown File Type dialog box. Click Save File to continue the download.

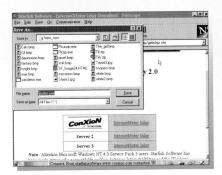

4 The browser displays the Save As dialog box when it is about to download the software. Leave the file name as is, and choose a temporary folder in the Save In drop-down list. If you download software or other files frequently, it's a good idea to create a folder named TEMP or DOWNLOAD for storing files off the Internet. On the other hand, saving to your Desktop places the file in an easy-to-access, easy-to-find location. Click OK to begin the transfer.

5 Navigator displays the Saving Location dialog box, just as it does when you save individual Web pages. This dialog box gives you a rough estimate of how much time the download will take.

How to Install Downloaded Files

If you haven't already done so, use the instructions on the preceding page to download the Starfish InternetMeter program into a temporary folder on your hard disk. Then close all programs before following these steps to install the software on your computer.

1 If the file you downloaded has a .ZIP extension, use WinZip to extract the setup files into the same temporary folder, and then go to step 4. (If you're not familiar with WinZip, see the tip in the FYI list on this page.)

InternetMeter

● WinZip is a shareware program for creating and opening files compressed in the .ZIP format. It is a must-have if you frequently download files from the Internet or send documents via e-mail. WinZip is available at http://www.winzip.com.

● If you don't like a program you've downloaded, then it's best, in an effort to save disk space, to uninstall it. Click on the Start button, point to Settings, and click on Control Panel. Double-click on Add/Remove Programs, select the program name in the Install/Uninstall tab, and click on the Add/Remove button. If you don't see the program name listed in this dialog box, click on the Cancel button and look for a file in the program folder called uninstall.exe. Double-click on this file and follow the instructions. If neither of these options work, you can delete the program's directory using File Manager.

7 Here is the newly installed InternetMeter running in the Internet Explorer window.

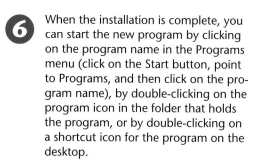

6 When the installation is complete, you can start the new program by clicking on the program name in the Programs menu (click on the Start button, point to Programs, and then click on the program name), by double-clicking on the program icon in the folder that holds the program, or by double-clicking on a shortcut icon for the program on the desktop.

2 Most program files that you download, including the one shown here, have an .EXE extension. Double-click on the .EXE file to see what happens. Some executables automatically extract the files they contain and then launch the installation procedure. If you see a message about starting setup or installation, you have an .EXE file of this type, and you can skip to step 5. Otherwise, go to the next step.

3 Double-clicking on the .EXE file may extract the files without starting the setup program. This type of .EXE file usually uses a DOS-based extraction program, so after you double-click on the file, you might see a DOS window as the files are being extracted. When the extraction is complete, you'll see the word Finished in the title bar of the DOS window. Click on the Close button in the upper-right corner of the window to close it.

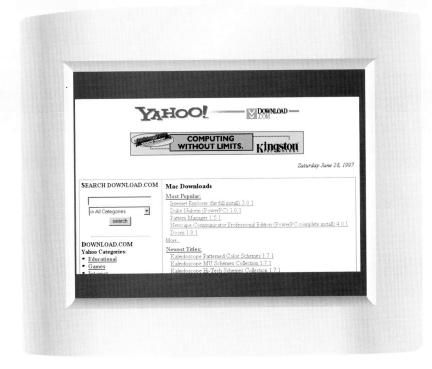

4 The extracted files often appear in the same folder as the original file. (If you unzipped a .ZIP file, the extracted files should also be in this same folder.) Look for a file called Setup.exe or Install.exe, and double-click on it to start the installation process.

5 Follow the on-screen prompts to complete the installation. The questions will vary depending on the program you're installing. As part of the installation, most programs create a new folder and install themselves into it.

What Is FTP?

Back when the Web was merely a gleam in a programmer's eye, people were already downloading files from Internet computers using a protocol called *FTP* (File Transfer Protocol). Now that the Web has become so popular, many companies make files available for downloading at their Web sites. However, individuals and companies have continued to use FTP because it is often the most convenient way to transfer files between computers on the Internet.

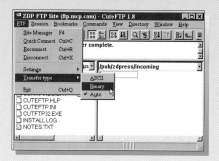

1 FTP lets you send binary files easily, and even computers that don't have Web server or browser support can usually handle FTP.

● Navigator and Internet Explorer don't handle FTP as well as some stand-alone FTP programs do, so if you use FTP frequently, you might want to get a shareware FTP program such as CuteFTP or WS_FTP (both available through http://www.tucows.com).

2 FTP uses FTP-client software built into your browser to retrieve or send files between your computer and host computers running FTP-server software. (These computers are commonly called FTP sites.)

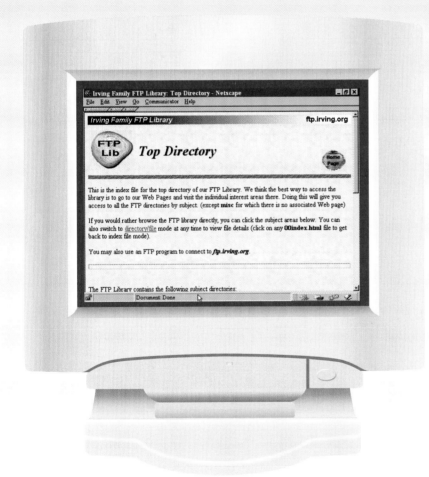

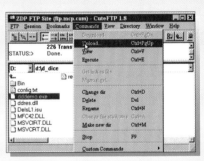

3 In addition to downloading files—including programs, graphics, text documents, and so on—from FTP sites around the world, you can upload files to FTP sites.

4 There are plenty of situations in which this comes in handy. For example, if you maintain your own Web site at your ISP, FTP is the easiest way to copy the Web pages you create on your own computer onto your ISP's computer.

How to Connect to an FTP Site

To connect to an FTP site, you need to know the name of an account on the FTP server. In other words, you need to log in with a user name and password so that the server knows who you are. Publicly accessible FTP sites expect you to use a special account called *anonymous*. Unless you tell Navigator otherwise, it assumes that you want to connect to FTP sites as an anonymous user, and it supplies the server with the user name *anonymous* and a password consisting of your own e-mail address. If you have a personal account on a host computer (your ISP, for example), you'll want to log onto the computer's FTP server using this account, because it will give you access to files that are not available to anonymous users.

1 Clicking on an FTP site link in a Web page is one way to connect to an FTP site as an anonymous user. If the URL in the status bar begins with *ftp://* the link points to an FTP site. (All URLs for FTP sites begin this way.) In this example, the link points to the Borland FTP site.

7 Navigator displays the FTP site, and the server places you in your home directory, to which you probably have rights.

● A company with an established FTP site may still be in the process of putting up their Web site, so their FTP resources may not all be available via the Web.

● Universities and other public institutions often maintain large FTP archives. You can search for FTP sites using the search services described in Part 4.

6 When you log into an FTP site using a personal account, the host computer prompts you for a password. Type it in and click OK. (Sending your password this way can be a security risk. Some stand-alone FTP programs avoid sending your password and use other, more secure ways to verify who you are to the server.)

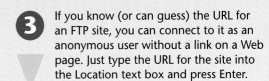

3 If you know (or can guess) the URL for an FTP site, you can connect to it as an anonymous user without a link on a Web page. Just type the URL for the site into the Location text box and press Enter.

2 Clicking on the link displays the FTP site. (You'll find out how to navigate in an FTP site on the next page.)

4 If you typed the URL correctly, Navigator connects to the requested FTP site, and the FTP server places you in the top-level directory of the area on the host computer to which anonymous users have rights.

5 To log into an FTP server using a personal account, insert your user name in the URL just after the *ftp://*. For example, I typed the URL **ftp://spidey@nuvotross.com** to log into a fictitious computer named *nuvotross.com* with a user name of *spidey*.

How to Navigate in an FTP Site

The directory structure at FTP sites is similar to the organization of folders on your hard disk. In many cases, anonymous users can download files stored in a directory called */pub* and its subdirectories, and can upload files to a directory called */incoming*. If you log into an FTP server with a personal account, you'll usually be given access to a personal directory—called your *home* directory—and its subdirectories.

Current directory is /

Welcome to the UMass-Lowell Archives

 1 The current directory is always displayed at the top of the screen with forward slashes (/) separating the levels of the directory structure, and the contents of the directory are listed underneath. Navigator uses various page icons to represent different types of files; yellow folder icons represent subdirectories.

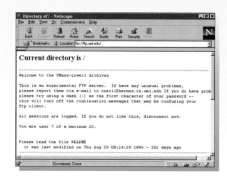

 6 If you continue to click on the Up to Higher Level Directory link, you eventually reach the top-level directory to which you have been granted access. This directory is indicated by a single forward slash (/).

● Sometimes administrators hide files for security reasons, so directories that appear to be empty may in fact contain files.

● If you try clicking on a directory to which you haven't been granted access, Navigator displays a message box telling you that it is unable to find that file or directory.

Please read the file README
it was last modified on Thu Aug 29 08:24:29 1996 - 302 days ago

Babylon-5/   Fri Jun 27 03:00:00 1997 Directory
README   580 bytes Thu Aug 29 00:00:00 1996

2 When you first arrive, click on links for any Readme or Welcome files. These usually list what materials are stored at the FTP archive and the various directories' contents. FTP and Web resources frequently overlap, so you can often access Web pages from an FTP server and FTP resources from a Web page. You can read either the HTML or plain text version of the Readme and Welcome files.

3 When you're done reading the Readme file, click on the Back toolbar button.

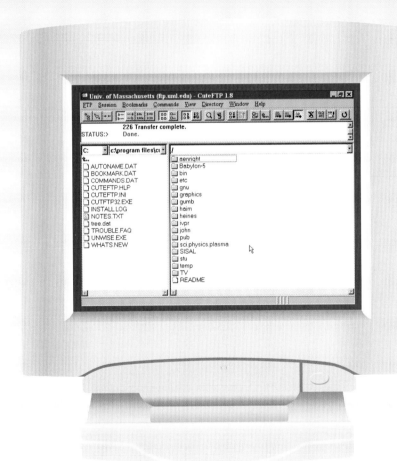

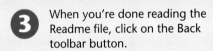

Babylon-5/   Fri Jun 27 03:00:00 1997 Directory

4 To move to a subdirectory, click on its link.

5 Netscape displays the contents of the sub-directory. To move back up to the previ-ous directory, click on the Up to Higher Level Directory link at the top of the list.

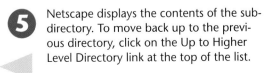

How to Download Files from an FTP Site

To find out about any operating system, hardware, or software requirements, read the relevant Readme documents before you download a file. To avoid viruses, download files from reputable FTP sites, and check downloaded programs with antivirus software before installing them.

1 Display the directory that contains the file you want to download.

● Many FTP sites contain files that are compressed in the .ZIP format. WinZip can unzip these files for you.

● Other shareware FTP programs let you transfer files more efficiently than you can with Netscape Navigator. For example, CuteFTP (http://www.cuteftp.com) lets you drag and drop files between your computer and the FTP server. You can upload or download several files at once, and if you're connecting using a personal account, CuteFTP can remember your user name and password and supply it to the server.

6 Once you've saved the file, you can open it using the appropriate software. Here is a downloaded file, opened in a shareware graphics program called Paint Shop Pro.

2 To save the file to disk without first displaying it in the browser window, Shift+click on the link for the file, and then skip to step 4. You can also display the file in the browser window first. To do this, click on the link for the file, and then go to the next step. Since it only recognizes certain file types, Navigator may not display the file properly.

3 Navigator successfully displays the .JPG file in this example. Frequently, however, the file will not be a type that your browser can display properly, in which case it will either display an empty window or a bunch of garbage characters. If you have displayed the file and want to save it, choose File, Save As. (Even if Navigator doesn't display the file correctly, you can still save it with File, Save As.)

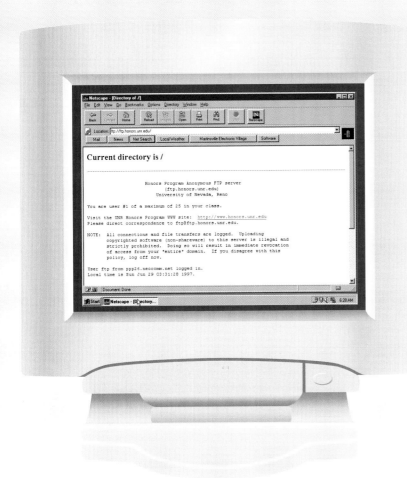

5 Navigator displays the Saving Location dialog box as it's saving the file.

4 In the Save As dialog box, choose a folder for the file in the Save In drop-down list, keep the existing file name, and click on the Save button.

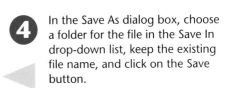

How to Upload a File to an FTP Site

Uploading to a company FTP server is often the quickest way to send a file, especially a binary file. For instance, if the file's recipient can't receive binary e-mail attachments, perhaps you can transfer the file, via FTP, to the recipient's company computer.

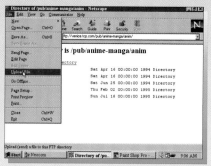

1 Connect to an FTP site and move to the directory where you want to upload your file. If you're using anonymous FTP, you will probably upload the file into the /incoming directory.

6 As soon as it finishes uploading the file, Navigator displays a message box telling you that the upload was successful. Click OK .

● If you try to upload a file to a directory to which you don't have write access, Navigator tells you that it could not post the file, and suggests that you may not have permission to write to this directory. If this happens, tell the system administrator, who will either modify the rights to that directory or suggest a different directory for you to use.

2 Choose File, Upload File to display the File Upload dialog box.

3 Navigator assumes you want to upload a Web page (an HTML document). If you want to upload a different type of file, select the type in the Files of Type drop-down list. If you want to see all of the files, choose All Files (*.*).

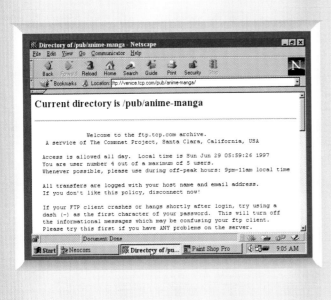

4 Use the Look In drop-down list to display the folder that contains the file, click on the file name, and click on the Open button.

5 Netscape displays a message box telling you it's uploading the file.

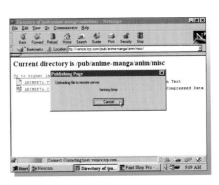

What Is Telnet?

Before the explosion of information Web technology, Telnet was a significant player in online information systems. Average folks used Telnet to connect to databases at libraries, universities, and scientific institutions; computer technicians used it to log into remote computers and troubleshoot problems.

1 Although computer gurus still use Telnet, most people have abandoned it in favor of the Web. Some resources, however, are still available only via Telnet.

2 Unfortunately, many remote applications to which Telnet links have text-based commands and a clunky interface.

3 Like FTP, Telnet is a client/server application. Your computer uses a Telnet-client program to connect to a remote computer running a Telnet-server program.

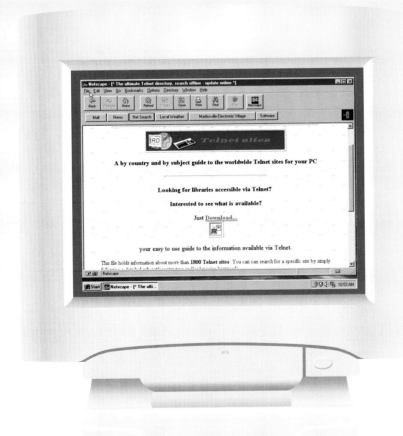

4 During a Telnet session, your computer functions as a terminal connected to the remote computer: You can type commands at your keyboard that the server computer responds to as if you were typing into its own keyboard.

How to Set Up Netscape Navigator to Use Telnet

Configuring Navigator to use the Windows 95 Telnet program is a simple process. After you've completed the steps on this page, Navigator automatically launches the Telnet program and attempts to connect to the remote computer whenever you jump to a Telnet site.

1 Choose the Options, General Preferences command in Navigator to display the Preferences dialog box.

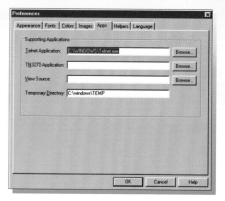

5 Now the Apps tab of the Preferences dialog box lists the path and file name of the Telnet application. Click OK to close the dialog box.

● You can configure Navigator to use any Telnet program you like, and there are several good third-party programs available at such software archives as Tucows (http://www.tucows.com). However, the Windows 95 Telnet application probably has all the capabilities you need.

● You don't have to open Navigator to use Telnet. Just establish a connection to your ISP, and then start the Telnet application. If you use Telnet independently of Netscape, you might want to create a shortcut for the program on your desktop.

2 Click on the Apps tab at the top of the dialog box.

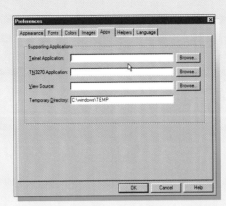

3 Clicking on the Browse button to the right of the Telnet Application text box displays the Select a Telnet Application dialog box.

4 The Telnet program is stored in your Windows folder. Use the Look In drop-down list to display the contents of the Windows folder, click on the file named Telnet.exe (depending on your Windows 95 configuration, you may not see the .EXE extension), and click on the Open button.

How to Connect to a Telnet Site

You can connect to a Telnet server by using the methods described here. After connecting, the Telnet server will request a login name. If you're connected to a public site, the name will either be listed in the resource used to locate the site (a book or a Web site, for example) or on the initial screen displayed. Public sites usually don't require passwords. If, however, you're connecting to a personal account, you will need to enter your regular user name and password.

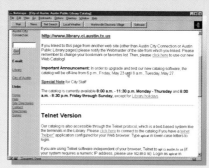

1 One way to connect to a Telnet site is to click on a link to a Telnet URL in a Web page. (All Telnet URLs begin with *telnet://*). The URL shown here points to Austin, Texas public library.

● When you're finished with a Telnet session, log off the remote computer. The commands for logging off vary from site to site; however, the most typical command on UNIX systems is *logout*. (Others are *exit, quit,* and *bye*.) If you can't decide what command to type, you can choose Connect, Disconnect to terminate the connection. You should only use this option as a last resort, however, because it may not properly close your session on the remote computer.

● Some Telnet servers require that you connect to a nonstandard port on the remote computer. If this is the case, you will see a colon followed by the port number at the end of the URL. If you're using the Connect dialog box to establish the connection, type the port number in the Port list box.

● The Telnet client and server programs must agree on what type of terminal your computer emulates. The default type is VT100, which usually works fine. If you need to change the terminal, choose a different type from the TermType list in the Connect dialog box.

7 Telnet makes the connection and prompts you for a login name.

6 Type a new Telnet site into the Host Name box (omitting the telnet:// at the beginning of the URL), leave the Port and TermType settings as is, and click on the Connect button.

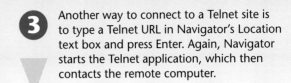

3 Another way to connect to a Telnet site is to type a Telnet URL in Navigator's Location text box and press Enter. Again, Navigator starts the Telnet application, which then contacts the remote computer.

2 Navigator launches the Telnet program, which starts a Telnet session with the remote computer. Note that because this Telnet site is open to the public, it tells you what to enter as your login name.

4 One other way to connect to a Telnet site is to launch the Telnet program first, and then contact the site. This method is convenient if you're contacting a site you've already visited, because the Telnet program keeps track of sites you've previously visited and lets you choose them with a click of the mouse. Begin by typing **telnet:** in the Location text box and pressing Enter.

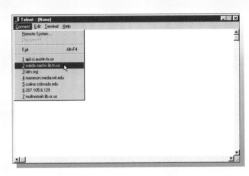

5 After Navigator starts the Telnet program, display the Connect menu. The sites you've visited recently are displayed at the bottom of the menu. If you see the one you want, click on it to create the connection. If the site isn't listed, choose Remote System to display the Connect dialog box.

How to Navigate in a Remote Application

During a Telnet session, you can issue commands to your local Telnet-client program by clicking on menu options. However, there is no consistent set of keyboard commands for navigating in every remote Telnet application (although Telnet applications do have a consistently unattractive interface). The best approach is to read the on-screen instructions carefully, and proceed slowly.

1 This Web page is part of the Web site for the Multnomah County Library in Portland, Oregon (http://www.multnomah.lib.or.us). Clicking on the Connect to DYNA link takes you to the library's online catalog. When you point to the link, Netscape displays a Telnet URL in the status bar. The Web page reminds you that you need a Telnet client to use the service, indicates what login name to use (*fastcat*), and tells you to type the name in lowercase letters.

7 The status of *Hammerstrike* is displayed. After reading the information, you can return to the Main Search Menu shown in step 3 by typing **R** and pressing Enter (for the Start Over command).

● If you don't see the characters you type on screen during a Telnet session, choose Terminal, Preferences, mark the Local Echo check box, and click OK. If you see two of each character you type, follow the same steps, but clear the Local Echo check box.

● If you want to save the contents of a Telnet session to a text file on disk, choose Terminal, Start Logging after you've started the session. In the Open Log File dialog box, choose a name and location for the file, and click on Open. From this point on, all that you see on screen is saved to the file you specified. When you want to stop logging, choose Terminal, Stop Logging.

6 The server displays detailed information about the book. Here, I entered **C** to get information about copy status.

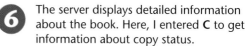

2 Clicking on the link launches the Telnet application and connects you to the remote computer. Type the login name at the prompt and press Enter.

3 After confirming you want to use VT100 terminal emulation (this is almost always correct) and quitting the library's news bulletin (by pressing Q and then Enter twice), the Main Search Menu pops on the screen. Type the number for the menu option you want and press Enter. Here, I typed **1** to search the catalog by title.

4 The Telnet server prompts you for a title, and I typed **Hammer's Slammers**, the title of one of my favorite military sci-fi novels.

5 Unfortunately, the librarians don't share my tastes, so the title was not included in the library's archives. Subsequently, I typed number **6** to get more information on *Hammerstrike*.

What Are Gopher Sites?

Gopher is yet another Internet navigation tool that has been eclipsed by the Web. Designed to help people locate resources on the Internet, Gopher lets you use a system of text-based menus to track down information.

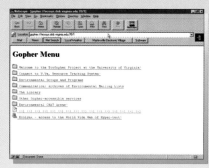

1 When navigating gopher menus, individual items point to resources (such as other gopher menus, FTP sites, Telnet sites, Web sites, and files) that are stored on the local system or on computers in some other part of the world.

● Although Web searches are usually quicker, and sufficient to locate most information you need, don't forget the gopher sites. Often they contain the same dusty nuggets of knowledge you'd find in a forgotten library corridor.

● Entering gopher in your favorite search engine's text box is a quick way to find gopher sites.

2 Gopher menus are stored on gopher servers, and you view them by using a gopher-client program.

3 Both Netscape Navigator and Microsoft Internet Explorer include a built-in gopher client and can access gopher servers when you click on their links in Web pages or type gopher URLs into the Location text box.

4 If you normally access the Internet through the Web, you won't have much need to deliberately search out gopher servers, since the search services on the Web are now the easiest means of finding Internet resources. However, you may stumble across gopher sites while you're browsing the Internet, so it's worth taking a quick look at them.

Visiting a Gopher Site

Connecting to and navigating in a gopher site is similar to visiting an FTP site. Both hold skads of information and present it in the clunkiest manner possible.

You can jump to a gopher site by clicking on a link in a Web page. This link leads to a gopher URL on United Nations Documents. As you might be able to guess by now, all gopher URLs begin with *gopher://*.

You can save the link as an HTML file or as plain text (*.txt). You can also save the file as the generic "All files" (*.*); however, you will have to designate a program to open it.

● A binoculars icon next to a menu item indicates that the file is a gopher index. Index files contain a search field you can use to search gopher menus for items containing particular keywords.

● You can print a document by clicking on the Print toolbar button.

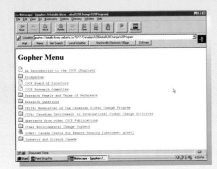

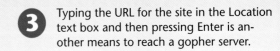

3 Typing the URL for the site in the Location text box and then pressing Enter is another means to reach a gopher server.

2 Clicking on the link displays the directory of folders. Navigator always displays the title *Gopher Menu* at the top of the screen when you're displaying a directory from a gopher server; Internet Explorer exhibits *Gopher directory*. The page icons next to menu items indicate that they are text files; computer monitors indicate Telnet sites; and folders represent directories.

4 Click on any folder link to display the submenu.

5 Right clicking on any "page" pops a shortcut menu that allows you to save the link.

PART 6

Security on the Internet

PERSONAL AND CORPORATE SECURITY are rapidly becoming an issue of prime importance on the Internet. From unintended viewers sneaking a peek at our e-mail, to malicious credit fraud, the Internet can be dangerously revealing.

Recently there have been instances of security breaches with both Netscape's and Microsoft's browsers. Moreover, the chink in both browsers' armor was found not by accident, or even by criminals with bad intent, but by hackers hoping to garner recognition for "breaking the code."

With this type of mentality existing in cyberspace, it's best to conduct your Internet business with an eye towards security. The next few pages will show you how to keep your transactions reasonably safe, your mail unread by unwanted peeping Toms (and Thomasinas), and your personal information secure.

IN THIS SECTION YOU'LL LEARN

- Security Issues on the Internet — 108
- Visiting a Secure Web Site — 110
- Downloading and Installing PGP — 112
- How to Send Secure Messages — 114
- How to Download and Install Security Certificates — 116
- How Companies Maintain Security — 118
- How to Shop on the Internet — 120
- How to Find Shopping Areas on the Web — 122
- How to Download and Install CyberPatrol — 124
- How to Download and Install Net Shepherd — 126
- How to Find Other Net-Filtering Programs — 128
- How to Protect Your Computer from Viruses — 130
- How to Get Comfortable with Cookies — 132

Security Issues on the Internet

When you transmit information across the Internet, there are several points where it could be intercepted. Sending a credit card number to an unsecure Web site is not as risky as leaving your wallet on the dashboard of an unlocked car on a busy Manhattan street, but it's close.

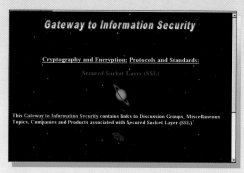

1 To address consumer security concerns, Netscape developed a protocol called Secure Sockets Layer (SSL). SSL lets Web servers encrypt data so snoopers cannot read the communications between the sender and receiver. We'll cover secure communications in greater detail later in this section.

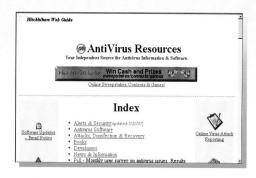

5 Download Internet files with caution. There are a lot of viruses out there, just waiting for a chance to infect your computer. We'll spend a couple of pages later on reviewing some tips for lowering the risk of getting infected.

● **Don't panic. Buying, selling, and sending stuff on the Internet is not a death-defying endeavor. Despite the semi-dark picture this chapter paints, Internet transactions are safe, providing you take the proper precautions.**

2 Companies that use the Internet normally keep private data and software on their internal network secure, while allowing employees access the Internet. In the next few pages you'll learn a few strategies for protecting internal information from potential Internet intruders.

3 The Internet is the world's largest, and most convenient, mall. Unfortunately, for the unwary, it can also be the most dangerous, due to information theft and fraud. We'll show you how to minimize your vulnerability to those risks.

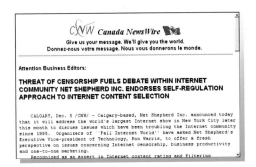

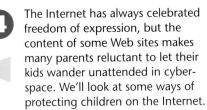

4 The Internet has always celebrated freedom of expression, but the content of some Web sites makes many parents reluctant to let their kids wander unattended in cyberspace. We'll look at some ways of protecting children on the Internet.

Visiting a Secure Web Site

Although secure sites represent only a small percentage of the total number of commercial sites on the Web, the number is growing rapidly. You can conduct a wide variety of secure business transactions over the Web, from making plane reservations to buying flowers, and soon, secure sites will become much more common.

1 As you know, the URLs for Web pages on standard (unsecure) servers begin with *http://*. Netscape Navigator also displays a broken key on a gray background in the lower-left corner of your screen to indicate that a page is unsecure. Here you see the standard (unsecure) home page for BeHOME, a home furnishing business that takes orders over the Web.

● Many sites contain mixed-security pages— secure pages that include unsecure sections. When you request one, Navigator displays a message box explaining that parts of the page are unsecure.

● Netscape Navigator 3.0 can store personal certificates and site certificates (Options, Security Preferences). A personal certificate (also called a digital ID) verifies your identity to others. If you visit a secure site that requires a personal certificate (most don't), your browser will automatically send the certificate for you. If you need a personal certificate, you can get one from Verisign (http://www.verisign.com). We'll cover this in "How to Download and Install Security Certificates."

● A site certificate verifies the identity of a remote Web site to you. When you connect to a secure site, the server sends the company's site certificate to your Netscape browser, and the browser confirms that it's valid before letting you browse the secure site.

7 When you click on a link in a secure page that points to an unsecure page, Navigator displays a message to let you know that a third party could observe any information you send to or receive from the requested page.

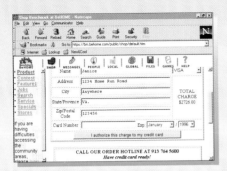

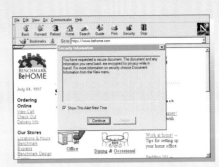

2 URLs for secure Web pages begin with *https://*. This is what BeHOME's home page looks like if you retrieve the page from BeHOME's secure server.

3 When you click on a link for a secure Web page or enter its URL in the Location text box, Netscape Navigator displays a message notifying you that any information you send or receive from the page will be encrypted. Click on the Continue button.

Document: Done

4 Navigator now displays the secure version of BeHOME's home page. You can tell a page is secure because you see an unbroken key icon on a blue background. In addition, Navigator displays a blue color bar across the top of the content area.

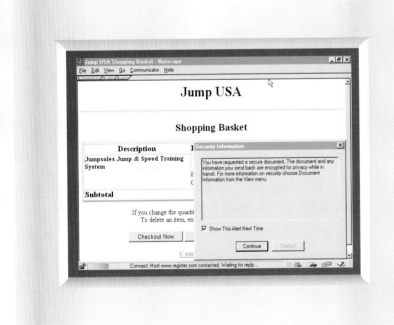

5 To find out more about the security status of a Web page, choose View, Document Info.

6 Navigator displays the Document Info window. The top pane displays information about the structure of the page, and the lower pane contains security information. The Security line defines the page's security level, and the Certificate information explains who is vouching for the identity and potential security of the site. (Most companies who run a secure server obtain a site certificate from a certifying authority confirming the identity of the company.) Close the window when you have finished reviewing the information.

Downloading and Installing PGP

We live in an open society but, nevertheless, most everyone has something they would rather someone else didn't know. Be it your credit card number, the name of your second girlfriend or boyfriend, or the outline for next month's business presentation, we all have secrets.

Pretty Good Privacy (PGP) software is encryption software that will encode and decode your e-mail and file transmissions. Originally freeware, PGP now comes with a price sticker on its box; however, you can still test drive a trial version before you buy.

PGP for Personal Privacy, Version 5.0 - Trialware

PGP for Personal Privacy, Version 5.0 builds on the heritage of PGP, which was originally

 Sneak over to the PGP site (http://www.pgp.com) to download the trial version of PGP 5.0.

● **You may, using PGP, encrypt a file on your computer that you do not wish others to access, even if you are not mailing it. Check the PGP Help file for details.**

● **Close all programs before installing PGP. Yes, that is standard advice, but this is one piece of software that will normally not install while other applications are running.**

 Follow PGP's instructions to create a default set of encryption keys. Turn to the next topic to learn how to send encrypted e-mail.

2 Before you may download, PGP requires confirmation that you live in the United States or Canada, are not a crook, and will not distribute the software outside the U.S.

3 Click on the 50trial-7911376.exe file to install PGP. Let the install Wizard walk you through the installation, but make sure you install all relevant applications.

4 If you wish to read the provided manual, you'll have to download a copy of Adobe Acrobat Reader from Adobe's site (http://www.adobe.com/supportservice/custsupport/download.html).

How to Send Secure Messages

O kay, now that you have the software down-loaded and installed, let's move on to sending the encrypted message. These pages will show you how to send messages using PGP.

1 Sending mail through Microsoft Exchange is a snap. First, type your e-mail as you normally do.

● Each PGP has two encryption keys: public and private. The public key, which you distribute to friends, family, and business colleagues, provides the data necessary for others to send you en-crypted e-mail. It does not provide the informa-tion that would allow others to decode messages sent to you. Only the private key allows you to decode your messages.

● Message security matters. Each e-mail sent passes through several servers. Technicians at any of these locations could read, and tamper with, the e-mail. PGP prevents this and keeps your private thoughts private.

8 Return to your e-mail application, paste the now-encrypted Clipboard contents into the application, delete the old text, and send your e-mail.

7 The PGP Key Selection dialog box will appear. Drag the name of the recipient to the Recipients box.

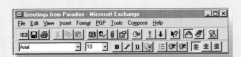

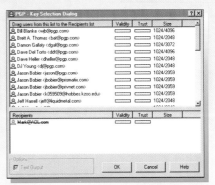

2 Next click on the Envelope/Lock button on the Exchange toolbar. The button will remain depressed.

3 Send the message. This will open the PGP Key Selection dialog box. This is a list of people who have sent the "public" portion of their key to the PGP server (see the FYI list for an explanation of public vs. private keys). Obviously, the person you wish to send the message to must either have mailed you their public key or have it posted here. Drag the recipient's name from the top of the Key Selection dialog box to the Recipients box at the bottom.

4 That's it. Whenever you are ready, you may transmit the message.

6 Right-click the PGP key on the Window's Taskbar and select Encrypt Clipboard.

5 The procedure is only slightly more complex for non-Exchange users. After typing your message, highlight the text and copy it to the Windows Clipboard using your e-mail editor's Edit, Copy command.

How to Download and Install Security Certificates

Digital identification, or security certificates, are the picture IDs of the Internet. Without them, you may be turned away from secure Web sites.

In their simplest form, they contain a name and public key. However, they frequently include the name of the certifying authority that issued the certificate, an expiration date, and a serial number.

 VeriSign is a popular company that offers digital IDs. Their Web address is **http://www.verisgn.com**.

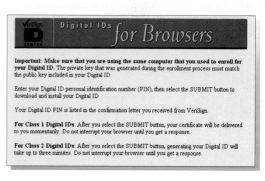

Report to the designated address and download your shiny new ID.

● You may set the level of security you want at the bottom of your Digital ID application. Be advised the better the security, the more memory it uses.

● Digital IDs are used by many applications, such as AOL, Microsoft Internet Explorer, and Netscape Navigator.

3 Click on the browser you wish to obtain the ID for. As VeriSign warns, IDs are valid only for the machines and software they were granted for.

2 Cruise over to their site and enter the download page. Click on the "Request an ID" button. Class 1 IDs, which provide the user with a specific name and e-mail address, are fine for casual browsing.

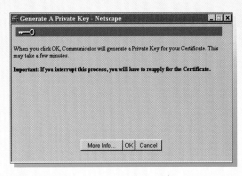

4 Confirm the type of ID you want. Then complete the form.

5 Once the form is completed, VeriSign generates your ID and sends you a confirmation e-mail.

Congratulations on obtaining a Trial Class 1 Digital ID(sm) from VeriSign!
As a Trial Digital ID holder, you join millions of users who can send
and receive secure e-mail using the built-in features of the latest
versions of Netscape, Microsoft, and other popular e-mail packages.
You also gain easy access to popular websites using your Digital ID
instead of passwords and one-step registration at websites requesting Digital IDs.

To assure that someone else cannot obtain a Digital ID that contains your
name and e-mail address, you must retrieve your Digital ID from

How Companies Maintain Security

Internet-connected companies want the advantages of Internet global communication but not the potential security problems. Most firms use a combination of the strategies discussed here to prevent intrusions and unauthorized transmissions.

1 Building a firewall is the most common way to protect sensitive material on a company LAN. A *firewall* is a cyberbarrier between the company's network and the Internet.

● As Internet traffic increases, so does the consumption of bandwidth, which often results in slower access times. For this reason, some Internet service providers and companies who otherwise wouldn't need firewalls set up Web proxies to take advantage of a proxy's ability to cache documents and hence speed up access times for frequently requested documents.

● If your computer is behind a firewall, there may be restrictions on what parts of the Internet you can access and what files you can download. The boss usually frowns on unauthorized Quake deathmatches on company time.

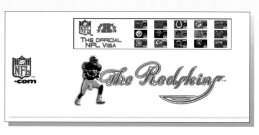

5 When companies put private corporate documents—such as company newsletters, training manuals, customer data, and product catalogs—on their intranet, employees can view them using a Web browser, but nobody outside the company can take a peek.

2 With a firewall, one computer serves as the *proxy*. Information, to and from the Internet, passes through the proxy, which evaluates it for potential security risks.

3 Proxies have another advantage: They can store Web pages that are frequently requested by employees in a *cache* (a temporary storage area). Since a proxy often provides a requested document from its own cache instead of retrieving the document from the Web, it speeds up document-access.

4 An intranet is another security option that many companies use. An *intranet* (or internal Web) is a private LAN or WAN running TCP/IP. Because intranets support HTTP, companies can set up Internet-type Web sites on them. Many intranets have no connection to the Internet.

How to Shop on the Internet

Security is a major concern when purchasing something through the Internet with a credit card, and although there are other ways to purchase goods and services online, the technology for securely transferring credit card numbers is normally as safe as shopping at the mall. The key for securely transferring credit card numbers, or other sensitive information, via the Internet is encryption technology. As you've seen, encryption simply means encoding information so that no one, other than the intended recipient, can decode the message. Without encryption, most of what you do on the Internet can be viewed by even inexperienced hackers.

1 One group using encryption technology is DigiCash, creator of ecash. *Ecash* is digital money—money that is stored and exchanged as digitized information through computer networks. The concept works in much the same way as withdrawing money from an ATM and then spending it at a local store. First, make a deposit at a bank that processes ecash. Then, using custom software, withdraw ecash and store it on your local computer. You can then spend this digital money at any shop accepting ecash, without having to open an account or transmit credit card numbers. DigiCash's URL is **http://www.digicash.com/**.

● **For a complete list of Internet resources on this topic, check out Commerce Introductory Material at http://gopher.econ.lsa.umich.edu/EconInternet /Commerce.html. This site includes links to many of the services mentioned in this section.**

● **Not to belabor the obvious...but be sure you check what encryption technology your Web Store uses. If it is unfamiliar to you, and you can't find any information on it, don't do business there.**

5 On the other hand, the SET standard will validate the WEB-supplier's/store's identification before providing credit card information, thus preventing fraudulent representation of merchandise. Additionally, all SET transactions are encrypted. For more information, ride your browser to **www.visa.com**.

2 CyberCash also provides encrypted transactions. Like ecash, CyberCash relies on custom software to encrypt and process a transaction. Unlike ecash, the CyberCash concept relies on the secure transfer of credit card information. CyberCash's URL is **http://www.cybercash.com/.**

3 Some companies do not process their billing through the Internet. One such company is First Virtual. Before making a purchase, a customer opens a First Virtual account. When a buyer purchases and receives a digital product by downloading it to his or her computer, the seller informs First Virtual and provides information about the transaction, such as the price of the item and the buyer's First Virtual account number. First Virtual then asks the buyer, via e-mail, to confirm that he or she agrees to purchase the product. If the buyer confirms the purchase, then the transaction is recorded on the buyer's First Virtual account and First Virtual bills the buyer's designated credit card. First Virtual's URL is **http://www.fv.com/.**

4 In May of 1997, Visa International and MasterCard announced the development of a technical standard for protecting payment card purchases on open networks. This protocol—named SET (Secure Electronic Transaction)—includes digital certificates that verify that the actual cardholder is making the purchase. This, in turn, provides financial institutions, merchants, and vendors with a means of preventing credit card fraud.

How to Find Shopping Areas on the Web

While the kinks in the money-transfer process get smoothed out, dozens of new Web-based shopping areas are emerging to service the anticipated hordes of online shoppers. They offer a nice alternative to the crowds and parking problems attendant to shopping malls. (On the other hand, their holiday decorations are pretty boring.)

1 The Internet Shopping Network was one of the first successful Web shopping areas. This site leans heavily toward computer products, with daily deals on hard drives, modems, RAM, and so on, but it also features links to some well-known specialty stores offering everything from flowers to telephones. Their URL is **http://www.internet.net/**.

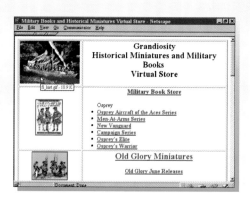

5 The Web is a haven for cottage industries and small business. Here's a fine example: The Grandiosity Historical Miniatures and Military Books Virtual Store is an online shop that specializes in military miniatures. Certainly not mainstream merchandise, but with the power of the Web, this modest business can reach billions of customers. Their address is **http://erinet.com/bp/index.html**.

● **Yahoo (http://www.yahoo.com) maintains a huge list of Internet shopping centers, as well as a variety of other business and commerce listings. The listing is alphabetical and includes many categories from advertising to vending machines. The directory path is Business and Economy: Companies.**

● **Don't forget, you can just search. Type what you are looking for (try +"internet mall") and see what turns up.**

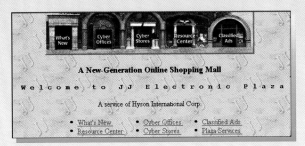

2 Some online shopping areas also provide a place for individuals to post "for sale" notices in newspaper want-ads style. Among these is JJ Electronic Plaza, which offers links to a bevy of vendors providing the obligatory computer products (hey, ya gotta eat, and ya gotta compute), as well as a few less obligatory items, such as rare and vintage record albums and underwater diving-mask lenses. Their URL is **http://www.jjplaza.com/**.

3 iMall, from Electronic Marketing Services, is an example of a Web-commerce environment that features stores set up to accept your purchases online. Many still rely on phone ordering though 800 numbers, but several iMall shops use some of the payment schemes presented in the previous topic for immediate and secure Internet purchasing. Check them out at **http://www.imall.com/**.

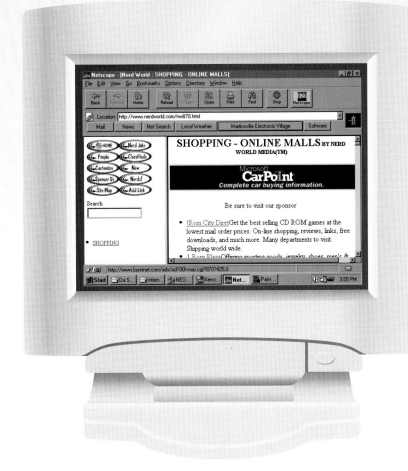

4 Of course, not all stores are located in shopping malls, and the same goes for cyberstores. The All-Internet site is among the resources offering links both to online malls and individual stores listed alphabetically by category. The categories cover everything you might expect, from arts to computers to health and beauty aids. The URL for All-Internet is **http://www.all-internet.com-/index-html/**.

How to Download and Install Cyber Patrol

Regardless of your views on censorship, if you're a parent and have Internet access at home, there are probably sites you prefer your children wouldn't browse. The next few pages discusses several popular site-blocking options, including Cyber Patrol and Net Shepherd.

1 Point your browser to the Cyber Patrol Web site (http://www.cyberpatrol.com). You can download a complete version of Cyber Patrol to test drive for a week. (When your week is up, you can either pay the piper or continue using a pared-down version.)

6 This is what a person will see if they attempt to access a blocked Web site.

● Ex-DOS users and File Manager gurus beware! The only safe way to uninstall Cyber Patrol is with the program's own routine. Anything else can cripple your browser. Now wouldn't you hate to lose all those bookmarks?

2 Download the software. Be sure to jot down the folder you save it to. ▶

3 Once downloaded, install the software following the on-screen prompts. During installation, the program will ask if you want a high- or low-security installation.

4 Cyber Patrol comes with a prede-fined list of blocked sites (including Web sites, FTP sites, newsgroups, games, and chat facilities) called the CyberNOT list. Categories in the list include violence, drugs, in-tolerance, and pornography. If you wish, you can customize the CyberNOT list by unblocking partic-ular categories or sites, or by adding specific sites to the list.

5 Cyber Patrol allows you to determine who uses your Internet applications, when they use them, and what they use them for. Additionally, Cybernet keeps a log of all sites visited.

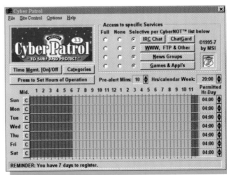

How to Download and Install Net Shepherd

All the Web filter applications we tested were excellent. Net Shepherd is a fairly recent addition to the fold and provides a full range of blocking routines in addition to some unique user filter routines. Unlike other blockers, Net Shepherd allows system administrators *and* users to vote on how objectionable they feel a site is.

1 Cruise over to the Net Shepherd home page (http://www.netshepherd.com) and download Net Shepherd. Please note, as of this publication's print date Net Shepherd did not support Internet Explorer 4.0 or Netscape Communicator 4.0.

● Net Shepherd uses the CRC rating system: General means that content is appropriate to all users; Child means that content is appropriate for ages 6-9; Pre-Teen content is appropriate for ages 10-12; Teen content is appropriate for ages 13-17; Adult content is appropriate for ages 18 and over; and Objectionable content—well, sky's the limit.

 This is what you will see if you land in a forbidden site.

2 During Net Shepherd's initial startup it will ask you, the administrator, to decide the levels of access for the users of your computers. You may allow them access to all sites but those that fall under the Adult and Objectionable (explicit content) categories, forbid real-time chatting, or limit access under a multitude of other options.

3 You may reset these options or add users later by clicking the Net Shepherd Administrator icon (in the Net Shepherd group).

4 Net Shepherd boots automatically when you start your computer. You must, however, click the Net Shepherd Login icon located on the Windows 95 toolbar or select Start, Programs, Net Shepherd, and log in to notify the Shepherd who is currently using the computer.

5 The program displays a rating bar at the

bottom of the screen. This bar rates each Web page visited for maturity of content and overall page quality. These values can be altered by vote (if so allowed) by all computer users. In other words, if, by mutual consent, a family feels a particular page does not contain adult content, they can vote to lower the rating to Pre-Teen.

How to Find Other Net-Filtering Programs

Cyber Patrol and Net Shepherd are only two examples of net-filtering software. There has been a veritable explosion of similar applications over the last couple of years. Here is a sample of the software you may chose from.

1 Cybersitter, like other filtering programs, allows the administrator (read parental-unit) to block or filter the Web sites, Usenet newsgroups, and chat lines that the other computer users have access to. Cybersitter comes with a "bad site" list 1,000 entries long, which can be updated with the click of a mouse. Point your browser to **http://www.cybersitter.com/** for additional information.

6 On the other side of the coin, Peacefire is a Web site and organization opposed to blocking software. The members of Peacefire do not condone violence, pornography, or vulgar language on the Internet. They do, however, believe it is the family's, not the software industry's, responsibility to monitor their children's use of the Internet.

● Although Net filters can be a useful tool, they do, like any other tool, need to be understood to be employed properly. Often innocent sites may be blocked due to the inclusion of terms such as "safe sex" on the Web page.

● Additionally, it is prudent to browse the sites your application blocks to ensure the sites are what you desire to be blocked.

2 SurfWatch is a widely known blocking program. The software comes complete with over 2,000 bad sites. Unfortunately, we couldn't find a downloadable demo. If you want to try SurfWatch, you'll have to cough up $49.95. You can find information on SurfWatch at **http://www.surfwatch.com/**.

3 Bess (http://bess.net) represents another kind of solution. To use Bess, you don't install software on your own computer. Rather, you subscribe to the service, which then becomes your "front door" into the Internet and the Web. Bess acts as a proxy, routing all communication between your computer and the Internet through its site.

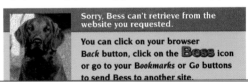

Bess Won't Retrieve That!

When a Bess subscriber tries to access a blocked site, they receive the following page instead of the one they requested. Clicking anywhere on the page returns them to the Bess home page.

Sorry, Bess can't retrieve from the website you requested.

You can click on your browser *Back* button, click on the Bess icon or go to your *Bookmarks* or *Go* buttons to send Bess to another site.

4 When you try to access a blocked site, Bess displays the page shown here. In addition to blocking pages, Bess provides an extensive set of links to Web resources for children and parents.

5 Rated-PG goes further than most other blocking applications. Rated-PG not only blocks the typical sites, newsgroups, and chat locations, but it can also limit what software is loaded on the computer and keeps an eye on game playtime. (After all, we wouldn't want those kids having any fun, would we?)

Welcome to Rated-PG!

Rated-PG by PCDataPower is the #1 choice to block X-Rated Internet Sites and limit playtime and installation of unwanted programs. Rated-PG is available for Windows 95.

Rated-PG supports all major online services such as America Online, CompuServe, and Prodigy as well as WWW Browsers, e.g. Netscape, Mosiac, NetCruiser...

How to Protect Your Computer from Viruses

A computer virus is a program that can replicate itself and subsequently spread from one computer to the next. Once a virus enters your computer, it may lie dormant, display messages, play sounds, damage data, or crash the computer. A virus may become active anytime your computer executes an infected program. While in memory, it can do considerable damage, including replicating throughout your computer and, if you're on a network, onto other network computers. When it comes to viruses, an ounce of prevention is worth a pound of cure.

1 Only download software from reputable sites. If a site is badly organized, has broken links or out-of-date material, or looks generally sloppy, the administrator of the site may not be taking proper precautions to avoid distributing software that contains viruses.

● File viruses are usually stored in program files and spread when you load the program. You can get this type of virus by downloading and installing infected programs from the Internet, or by getting an infected program from someone on floppy disks.

● Boot-sector viruses are stored in the boot sector of a disk. When you turn on your computer, it normally reads the boot sector of your hard disk. However, if you accidentally turn on your computer while an infected floppy is still in the drive, the computer will automatically boot up from the floppy, reading the boot-sector virus into memory.

● Macro viruses are relatively new. They infect document templates, such as Word or Excel templates, and from there they spread to every document you create based on the infected template. You can get macro viruses from documents people give you on floppies or from documents you receive as e-mail attachments. (You can't get viruses by reading plain-text e-mail.)

8 Both Norton AntiVirus and McAfee's VirusScan automatically load when you boot up, and run in the background. Antivirus programs can help you detect viruses, clean them off your system, and repair any damage. Keep in mind, however, that this software is by necessity one step behind the bad guys. McAfee and Symantec can't design a fix for a virus until someone reports the virus to the company, by which time it may have already caused someone grief.

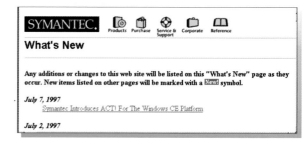

7 Symantec places monthly updates of Norton AntiVirus (which contain the latest antivirus routines) on their Web site. Just download the file and then double-click on it to install the update.

2 If you are uncertain whether a site is reputable, ask around in an applicable newsgroup. You'll usually get plenty of advice.

3 Because viruses are often spread on floppy disks, you should never use a floppy without scanning it first.

4 Back up your hard disk regularly. If a virus causes a major crash and data loss, at least you'll have some hope of salvaging your files.

5 There are two popular anti-virus programs. One is McAfee's VirusScan for Windows 95 (http://www.mcafee.com).

6 The other is Norton AntiVirus from Symantec (http://www.symantec.com).

How to Get Comfortable with Cookies

Cookies are perhaps the most misunderstood concept on the Web. No, we aren't talking about oatmeal or chocolate chip, but rather those that Web servers feed you—without the ice cold milk.

A cookie is a set of information a Web server sends that your browser retains and, later, returns to the Web server, usually when the user returns to the site.

1 Here's an example of a cookie in action: Say you visit an online store and, during your browsing, you fill your cybershopping cart—but then you leave without making a purchase. The cookie saves (on your computer) the information about your shopping trip, so that if and when you return to that store, those items will be right where you left them, albeit unpurchased, in the bottom of your cart.

6 In Internet Explorer, select Options under the View pull-down menu. Click on the Advanced tab, and check "Warn before accepting cookies."

● Cookies are not the only way Web servers garner information about your computer. Just visiting a Web site tells the server what type of browser you're using and your ISP address.

● Although cookies can be used to track where you move in a specific Web site, this information can also be gleaned by the Web master without using cookies.

2 Some sites use cookies to store your specific viewing preferences. For instance, if you direct a site to turn off its frames, the frames will remain off each time you return to the site.

3 Cookies are not the hirelings of some secret government agency hoping to discover your pet feeding habits. They can, however, show Web masters which pages you have visited, your e-mail address (only if you have previously supplied it to the site), and any other information you have knowingly supplied.

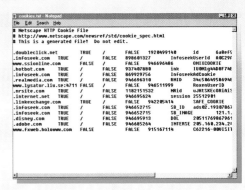

4 If you would like to view or delete your cookies, you can. They are located in the Netscape Navigator or Internet Explorer folder. Of course you'll have to do this after each session. Above is my cookie.txt file.

5 You may find out when a cookie is being offered to your system, and therefore block it if you choose, in both Netscape Navigator 3.0 and Internet Explorer. For Navigator, select the Network Preferences Menu from the Options menu, click on the Protocol tab, find the Alert Before section, and check the box labeled Accepting a Cookie.

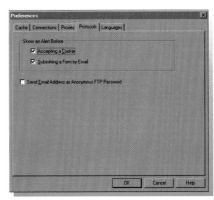

PART 7
E-Mail and Internet Communities

THE INTERNET is more than a collection of dazzling pages, Telnet, FTP, and Gopher sites. You can talk to the Web, and it will talk back. Employing the Web as a social tool is one of the most interesting uses of the medium.

From e-mail to Usenet newsgroups to real-time chat to online gaming, we'll take you on a tour of the Internet community and nudge you on your way to Netizenship.

IN THIS SECTION YOU'LL LEARN

- How to Send E-Mail with Netscape Mail   136
- How to Send E-Mail with Microsoft Exchange   138
- How to Handle Incoming E-Mail Messages   140
- How to Store E-Mail Addresses   142
- How to Reply to or Forward an E-Mail   144
- How to Attach a File to Your E-Mail   146
- How to Attach Multiple Files   148
- How to Save and Unzip an Attachment   150
- How to Choose a Mailing List   152
- How to Subscribe to a Mailing List   154
- What Are Newsgroups?   156
- How to Search Newsgroups with Deja News   158
- How to Subscribe to a Newsgroup   160
- How to Read Newsgroup Messages   162
- How to Interact with Newsgroups   164
- How to Post a Newsgroup Message   166
- How to Chat with IRC   168
- How to Use the Proper Chat Etiquette   170
- How to Use Voice-Aided Chat   172
- How to Game on the Internet   174
- Joining an Online Game Service   176
- How to Use MUDs   178

How to Send E-Mail with Netscape Mail

Writing and sending an e-mail message is straightforward: Type the e-mail address of the recipient, the subject line, and the body of the message, and then click the Send button. That's all there is to it. It doesn't matter if you are using Microsoft Exchange, Netscape Mail, or AOL. Throughout this section we'll focus on Netscape; however, the procedures are similar no matter which browser or online service you use. The steps on this page describe sending e-mail when you're connected to your ISP, but you can also compose messages offline, and then send them when you connect.

1 Click on the Mail icon in the lower-right corner of the Netscape window (or choose Window, Netscape Mail).

8 Type the body of the message, and then click on the Send button. After Netscape sends the message, it automatically closes the Message Composition window. If you are finished using e-mail, close the Netscape Mail window by clicking on its Close button.

- To see the messages you've sent, double-click on the Sent folder in the Mail Folder pane of the Netscape Mail window. You'll learn about the various panes in the Netscape Mail window a little later.

- You can easily switch from Netscape Mail back to the main Netscape window by clicking on Netscape's taskbar button.

7 If you wish, use the Attachment button to specify one or more attachments—either files or Web pages—to send with the message. (You'll learn about sending and receiving attachments in a few pages.)

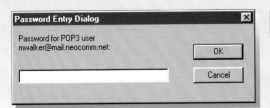

2 Netscape asks for your mail password, which is usually the same as the password you use to connect to your ISP. Type the password and click OK. (To avoid entering the password in the future, choose Options, Mail and News Preferences, click on the Organization tab, mark the Remember Mail Password check box, and then click OK.)

3 Netscape displays the Netscape Mail window. Click on the To:Mail toolbar button to display the Message Composition window. (You can also display the Message Composition window from the main Netscape window by choosing File, New Mail Message or by pressing Ctrl+M.)

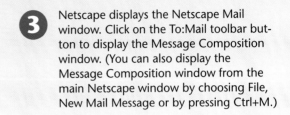

4 Type the recipient's e-mail address in the Mail To text box. To send the message to several people, type all their e-mail addresses, separated by commas. If you use Netscape's address book, you can save yourself some typing by clicking on the Mail To button (or the Address toolbar button) and selecting the recipient from the Select Addresses dialog box. (See "How to Store E-Mail Addresses" later in this section.)

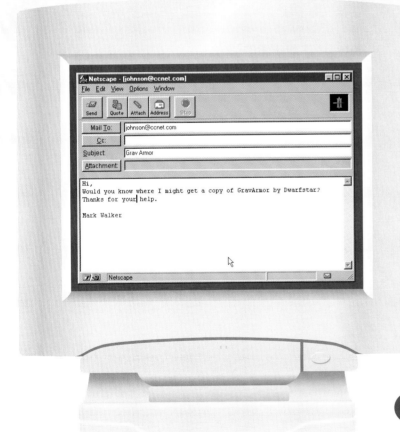

5 If you want to send copies of this message to one or more people, type the appropriate e-mail addresses in the Cc text box. If you want to send blind copies, choose View, Mail Bcc to add the Bcc text box to the Message Composition window, and then type the e-mail addresses in the Bcc text box. (Mail To and Cc recipients won't see the names of Bcc recipients. Bcc recipients will see the names of the Mail To and Cc recipients, but they won't see the names of the other people to whom you sent blind copies.)

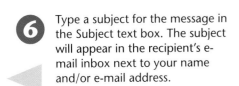

6 Type a subject for the message in the Subject text box. The subject will appear in the recipient's e-mail inbox next to your name and/or e-mail address.

How to Send E-Mail with Microsoft Exchange

As we said before, sending e-mail is simple, and the process is pretty much identical no matter which browser you use. There are, however, a few differences in the various browser and online services e-mail interface. Here, we'll teach you how to shoot off a message with Microsoft Exchange.

1 Double-click on the Inbox icon on the desktop.

● Understandably, Internet Explorer's e-mail routine is similar to Exchange. To e-mail from Explorer, select Mail, New Message from the Internet Explorer window. Type the message, fill in the To line (clicking on the address book will open your personal address book), and click Send. Again, you'll have to open Microsoft Exchange and run through step 5 to send the message.

● You can check your spelling in Microsoft Exchange by selecting Spelling from the Windows Messaging Tools Window. Who would have ever thunk the computer would replace a dictionary? (oops)

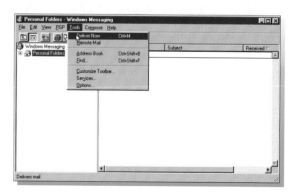

5 To send—I mean no-kidding send—the mail, pull down the tools menu and choose Deliver Now. Once the mail is sent, it will disappear from your outbox.

2 Once Exchange pops onto your screen, tap the New Message icon in the toolbar.

3 Type the recipient's name in—you guessed it—the To box. Alternatively, click on the Address book icon, select the address book you wish to use, choose the name of the recipient, and click To.

Send button

4 Type the subject and message, and click the Send button (the yellow "in motion" envelope). This stage, however, is when it gets a tad tricky, because clicking Send does not send the message. Read on.

How to Handle Incoming E-Mail Messages

O nce you've read e-mail, you can leave it in your inbox indefinitely; however, your old messages will be easier to find if you periodically clean house, deleting unwanted messages and moving useful e-mail into other folders. Again, while not identical, Netscape Mail and Internet Explorer share similar filing functions.

1 Netscape displays an exclamation point next to the Mail icon in the lower-right corner of the Netscape window when new messages are waiting on your ISP's mail server. Click on the icon to display the Netscape Mail window and retrieve the messages.

8 To print a message, click on it in the Message Header pane, click on the Print toolbar button, then click on OK in the Print dialog box.

● You can resize the panes in the Netscape Mail window by dragging the gray borders that separate them.

● You can delete several messages at a time by selecting all the messages before pressing the Delete key. To select adjacent messages, click on the first message and then Shift+click on the last message. To select nonadjacent messages, click on the first one and then Ctrl+click on all the additional messages.

● By default, Netscape sorts messages according to date. To change the sort order, click on the gray buttons at the top of the Message Header pane. For example, to sort in alphabetical order by sender, click on the Sender button.

● If your Inbox folder contains a lot of messages, you may want to flag the important ones so that you can come back to them easily. To do this, click in the column to the right of the Sender name in the Message Header pane to place a small red flag in the message header. You can jump between flagged messages by choosing the First Flagged, Next Flagged, and Previous Flagged in the Go menu.

7 The new folder appears in the Mail Folder pane. Drag the message from the Message Header pane and release the mouse when its over the folder. Netscape Mail moves the message from the Inbox folder to your newly created folder.

6 Type a name for the folder and click OK.

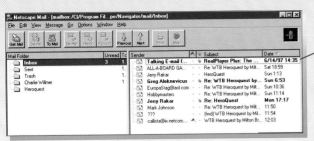

New message

2 As shown in the central graphic, the Netscape Mail window is divided into three panes. The Message Header pane displays the sender, the subject, and the date of each message in the Inbox folder, which is located at the top of the Mail Folder pane. New messages are boldfaced and marked with a green flag.

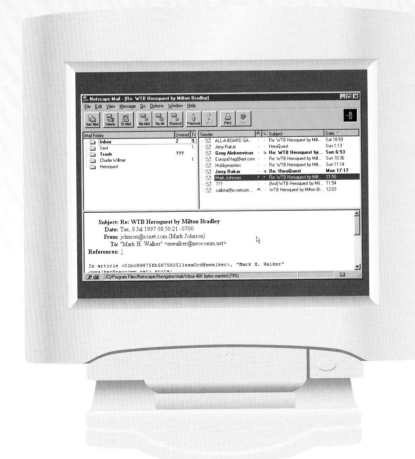

3 Click on a message to read it. The message is displayed in the Message pane at the bottom of the window. Use the vertical scroll bar to scroll the message.

4 To delete a message, select the message in the Message Header pane and click on the Delete tool-bar button or press the Delete key. Netscape Mail sends the message to the Trash folder. Until you empty the Trash folder (by choosing File, Empty Trash Folder), you can display any of the messages it contains.

5 If you want to store a message, first create a folder for it in the Mail Folder pane (if an appropriate folder doesn't already exist). To do this, choose File, New Folder. Note that the folders in the Mail Folder pane are visible only in Netscape; they aren't actual folders in Windows 95. Netscape puts all the information about these folders in Netscape\Navigator\Mail, but you don't need to deal with these files directly.

How to Store E-Mail Addresses

You can store e-mail addresses in Netscape Mail's address book or Exchange's Personal Address Book. Then, you can select the e-mail address from the address book instead of typing it. The Netscape Mail address book also lets you group people together in lists; you could create a list for your family members or for the members of your cult (just kidding). Just enter the name of the list in the Mail To text box, and Netscape Mail sends the message to everyone in the list.

1 If you want to store the e-mail address of someone who sent you a message, click on the person's message in the Message Header pane of the Netscape Mail window and then choose Message, Add to Address Book. This method is fast, but it doesn't store any information other than the person's e-mail address. If you have several addresses to enter, or if you want to enter more complete information about people, go to steps 2 and 3.

8 If you entered a nickname for a person or list in step 3, you can type the nickname in the Mail To text box. As soon as you press the Tab key or click in another part of the Mail Composition window, Netscape replaces the nickname with the name of the person or list, followed by the e-mail address or the full name of the list in brackets.

● When you click on a name in the Address Book window, Netscape displays the e-mail address for that person in the status bar at the bottom of the window.

● To edit an entry in the Address Book window, right-click on the entry and choose Properties from the context menu. To delete an entry, click on it and press the Delete key.

● To save an e-mail address in Microsoft Exchange, double-click on the message sender, then click on the address book (in the window that pops) you wish to save the address in.

7 Select the person or list you want, and tap the To button. If you're sending a message to multiple people, click on each address and then click the To, Cc, or Bcc button to have Netscape place the addresses in the appropriate text boxes. (Remember that the Bcc text box is not displayed by default. If you want to use it, first choose View, Mail Bcc in the Message Composition window.) Then click OK to close the dialog box.

2 To enter e-mail addresses directly into the address book, start by choosing Window, Address Book. (This command is available in the main Netscape Navigator window, the Netscape Mail window, and the Message Composition window.)

3 In the Address Book window, choose Item, Add User and then in the blank address book form fill in the Nickname, Name, E-Mail Address, and Description text boxes. (Step 8 explains what nicknames are for. The description isn't used outside the address book.) Click OK when you've completed the form. When you're finished editing the address book, click on the Close button in the upper-right corner of the Address Book window.

4 To create a list, start by choosing Item, Add List in the Address Book window. Select the default entry in the Name text box (New Folder) and replace it with the actual name of the list. Optionally enter a nickname and a description, and then click OK.

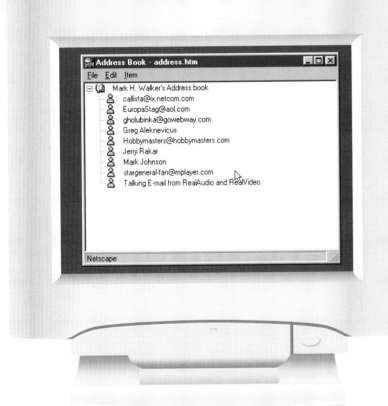

5 The new list is added to your address book. (Notice that Netscape uses book icons to indicate lists.) Now add e-mail addresses to the list by dragging and dropping them on the list name. Netscape leaves the e-mail addresses in their original locations in the address book and creates *aliases* (pointers to the actual entries) for the addresses in the list. When you're finished creating the list, close the Address Book window.

6 To use the address book, click on the Mail To button (or the Address button) in the Message Composition window to display the Select Addresses dialog box.

How to Reply to or Forward an E-Mail

Like other e-mail programs, Netscape Mail can reply to and forward messages. When you reply to a message, you don't have to retype the person's e-mail address or the subject line because Netscape fills in the information for you. The forward feature lets you pass a message on to someone else.

1 In Netscape Mail, start by clicking on the message in the Message Header pane. Then click on the Re:Mail toolbar button. In Exchange, click on the message, then the Reply icon.

- When using Microsoft Exchange, you can automatically include the original text in your reply. Select Tools, Options, Read. On the Read tab, click Include Original text when replying.

- If you want Netscape to always quote the original message in your replies, choose Options, Mail and News Preferences, click on the Composition tab, mark the check box labeled Automatically Quote Original Message When Replying, and then click on OK.

- If the message to which you're replying was sent to other people besides yourself, you might want to send your reply to both the sender and the other recipients. To do this, click on the Re:All button in Netscape, or click Microsoft Exchange's two-headed icon, instead of the Re:Mail button in step 1.

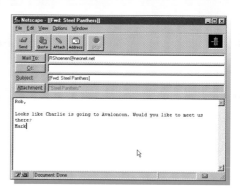

8 Enter the new recipient's address, type an introductory message if necessary, and hit the Send button.

7 To forward a message, click on the message you want to forward, and then click on the Forward button or icon.

Subject: **Re: WTB Heroquest by Milton Bradley**
Date: Sun, 06 Jul 1997 11:14:09 -0400
From: Hobbymasters <Hobbymasters@hobbymasters.com>
Organization: Hobbymasters
To: "Mark H. Walker" <mwalker@neocomm.net>
References: 1

2 Both Netscape Mail and Exchange display their Message Composition windows with the sender's e-mail address entered in the Mail:To text box and the original subject entered in the Subject text box. They preface the subject with *Re:* to let the recipient know that your message is a reply.

3 Type your message, and then click Send.

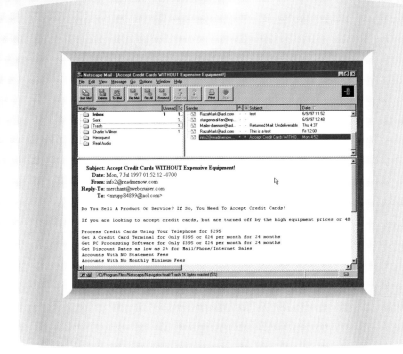

4 In e-mail correspondence, it is standard practice to quote portions of the original message in your reply to let the recipient know what parts of the original message you're responding to. To quote the original message, follow steps 1 and 2, and then, in Netscape Mail, click on the Quote toolbar button.

5 In Exchange, you will have to paste the text (using edit commands) or set the default options to automatically include the original text in a reply (check the FYI list).

6 Netscape inserts the original message in the Message Composition window, prefacing each line with the > symbol. Exchange indents the original if you so choose in the default settings. If you paste the original text into your reply, you must apply any special formatting yourself. Type your reply and click Send. See "How to Send E-Mail with Microsoft Exchange" to ensure you have properly sent your Exchange mail.

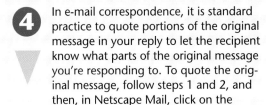

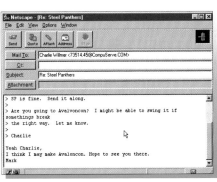

How to Attach a File to Your E-Mail

When you attach a document to an e-mail message, your browser sends an exact copy of the file to the recipient. At the receiving end, the recipient can open, edit, and print the file, just as if it had been created on his or her own computer.

By the way, if the receiver doesn't have the software to run the program, he won't be able to run it. So remember—that Word 97 file will be useless to someone running WordPerfect 5.1.

We'll focus here on Netscape Mail. However, the principles are the same for any e-mail application.

1 Display the Message Composition window (click To:Mail in the Netscape Mail window or choose File, New Mail Message from the main Netscape Navigator window), fill in the Mail To, Cc, and Subject text boxes, and type a message. Click the Attachment button (or click the Attach toolbar button) to display the Attachments dialog box.

● If you add a file in the Attachments dialog box and then decide you don't want to send it, click on the file name and then click on the Delete button. Netscape Mail removes the file name from the Attachments dialog box. (It doesn't, however, delete the file from your disk.)

● Attaching files in Microsoft Exchange is similar: Write a message, click on the paper clip (Insert) icon, choose your file from the Look In window, and click OK.

● If you're sending a file to someone who uses a Mac, either save it in Mac format (if the program you used to create the file uses different formats for Mac and PC files) or make sure the recipient can handle a Mac file. Sending a file over the Internet to a Mac computer does not automatically convert the file for use on a Mac.

6 Netscape Mail lists the name of the attached file in the Attachment box. (Since the Attachment box is gray, the file name may be hard to see.) Click on the Send button to send the e-mail message. Because Netscape Mail has to send a copy of the attached file, the message will take longer to send than messages with no attachments, and obviously the larger the attachment, the longer the transfer time.

2 Click on the Attach File button to display the Enter File to Attach dialog box.

3 Use the Look In drop-down list to display the folder containing the document you want to attach, select the file name, and click the Open button.

4 Netscape Mail displays the name of the file in the Attachments dialog box. If you want to add one or two more attachments, you can repeat steps 2 and 3 to add more file names to this dialog box. When you are sending more than one file, however, it is better to compress the individual files into one .ZIP file. (See "How to Attach Multiple Files to an E-Mail" later in this section.)

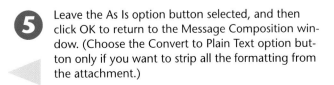

5 Leave the As Is option button selected, and then click OK to return to the Message Composition window. (Choose the Convert to Plain Text option button only if you want to strip all the formatting from the attachment.)

How to Attach Multiple Files

A shareware program called WinZip is a valuable assistant when sending a large number of files via e-mail. Using WinZip, you can compress the files into a single .ZIP file (also called an archive) and attach the .ZIP file to an e-mail message. If you haven't already done so, download and install WinZip. (The program is available at **http://www.winzip.com.**)

1 Start WinZip either by choosing it from the Start, Programs menu or by double-clicking on its shortcut icon.

7 Now follow all the steps in "How to Attach a File to Your E-Mail" earlier in this section, selecting the .ZIP file in step 3.

● It's even a good idea to compress single documents to reduce their upload and download time.

● If you add a file to a WinZip archive and then decide you don't want to include it, click on the file name in the WinZip window and press the Delete key. WinZip displays the Delete dialog box. Make sure the Selected Files option button is marked, and click on the Delete button. This removes the file from the archive but does not delete it from your disk.

6 WinZip compresses the selected files. This process can take from a few seconds to several minutes, depending on the number and size of the files. Once this batch of files is compressed, you can repeat steps 4 and 5 if necessary to add files from other folders. When done, click on the Close button in the upper-right corner of the WinZip window.

2 If you see the WinZip Wizard (a feature added in version 6.1), click on the WinZip Classic button to display the standard WinZip window, which we will be using in this example, and then click on the New button to display the New Archive dialog box.

3 Choose a location for the file in the Create In drop-down list, and type a name for the file in the File Name text box. (If you omit the .ZIP extension, WinZip adds it for you.) Then click OK.

4 Click on the Add button to tell WinZip which files you want to compress.

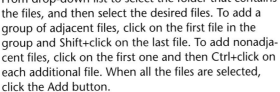

5 WinZip displays the Add dialog box. First use the Add From drop-down list to select the folder that contains the files, and then select the desired files. To add a group of adjacent files, click on the first file in the group and Shift+click on the last file. To add nonadjacent files, click on the first one and then Ctrl+click on each additional file. When all the files are selected, click the Add button.

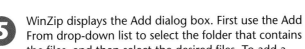

How to Save and Unzip an Attachment

Saving and unzipping an e-mail attachment is quick and easy. If you haven't already done so, you need to download and install the most recent Windows 95 version of WinZip (see Part 6 for help). The program is available at **http://www.winzip.com**.

Attachment link

Subject: Here is the file I promised
Date: Mon, 14 Jul 1997 17:27:42 -0400 (EDT)
From: RazaMark@aol.com
To: mwalker@neocomm.net

Hi Mark,
Here's the file for your book.
Ed

Part 1.2   Name: NONAME.ZIP
            Type: Zip Compressed Data (application/x-zip-compressed)
            Encoding: base64

1 To detach a .ZIP file that someone has e-mailed to you, click on the message with the .ZIP attachment and scroll to the bottom of the message and click on the attachment link.

● If you want Netscape Mail to launch WinZip automatically when you click on a link for a .ZIP file, choose Options, General Preferences, and click on the Helpers tab. Click on the line for application/x-zip-compressed, and click on the Launch the Application option button at the bottom of the dialog box. Next, click on the Browse button, and in the Select an Appropriate Viewer dialog box, find and click on the executable file for WinZip (Winzip32.exe, which should be in the WinZip folder). Click on the Open button, and then click on OK to close the Preferences dialog box.

● StuffIt is the compression program most widely used on the Mac. If you want to exchange compressed files with a Mac user, either you'll need to get the PC version of StuffIt, or the Mac user will have to get a compression program that can handle .ZIP files.

8 The Files option button in the Extract dialog box allows you to extract only files that match the criteria you type in the text box. In this example, *.xls* will extract only the Excel spreadsheet files, (bonus*.* would extract only files whose names begin with bonus, and so on).

Files
○ Selected Files
○ All Files
● Files: *.xls

7 Depending on the number and size of the files you're extracting, it can take from a few seconds to several minutes to extract them. WinZip shows you its progress at the bottom of the WinZip window. When it's finished, click on the Close button in the upper-right corner of the window to close the program.

2 If you see the Viewing Location message box, that means Netscape Mail is configured to start WinZip automatically whenever you click on a link to a .ZIP file, and you can skip directly to step 4.

3 If you see the Save As dialog box, Netscape is not configured to start WinZip automatically when it encounters a .ZIP file, so you need to manually save the file. Pick a folder for the .ZIP file in the Save In drop-down list, keep the existing file name, and click Save. Once the file is saved, double-click on the file to start WinZip.

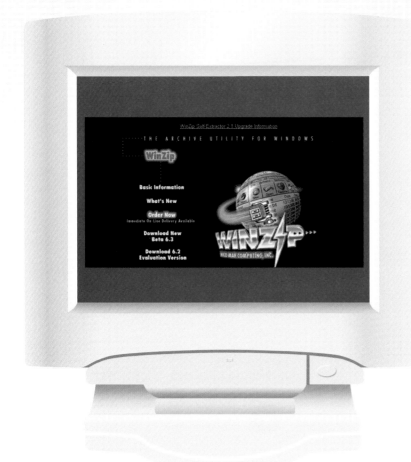

4 As soon as WinZip starts, it automatically decompresses the .ZIP file and lists all its component files in the WinZip window. You now have to tell WinZip which files you want to extract and where you want to put them. If you want to extract all the files, start by clicking on the Extract button to display the Extract dialog box.

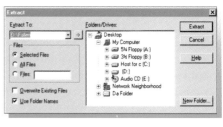

6 To extract only certain files, select them in the WinZip window before clicking on the Extract button. If you do this, the Selected Files option button in the Extract dialog box becomes active. Click on it to extract only the selected files. To extract files to more than one folder, just repeat this process, choosing a different folder in the Folders/Drives box each time.

5 The All Files option button is selected by default. This option tells WinZip to extract all the files in the .ZIP file. To do so, just choose a folder in the Folders/Drives box to hold the extracted files, and click on Extract. If you want to extract files to more than one folder, or if you want to extract only some of the files in the .ZIP file, continue with steps 6 and 7; otherwise, skip to step 8.

How to Choose a Mailing List

Like newsgroups, mailing lists are a forum for sharing thoughts, views, and advice. Unlike most newsgroups, however, many mailing lists are moderated, meaning that someone screens the contributions to ensure their content and tone are appropriate for the list.

There is no common "board" to post messages on. Your e-mail is sent, through a central administrator, to the other mailing list subscribers. Everyone receives your message, as well as any other submissions from list subscribers, as separate messages.

1 There is no single strategy for locating mailing lists. The best way to find private mailing lists is through word of mouth. Public mailing lists are easier to locate, especially if you use one of the many "lists of lists" on the Internet. The most extensive list of mailing lists is in the Liszt site at **http://www.liszt.com**.

● It's easy to subscribe to a mailing list found in Liszt's database. Read the information on how to subscribe, and then click on the link for the administrative address. Liszt displays the Message Composition window with the administrative address already entered in the Mail To text box. Type the subscription command and click on the Send button.

● If you want to start your own mailing list, a good place to begin gathering information is http://www.lsoft.com, the Web site of L-Soft International. This company distributes the Listserv software, which now includes a version for Windows 95.

[Intro ⁞ | Answers | Index | Search]

 Choose Subjects to search for mailing lists by topic. Click on a subject of interest to see a list of all the mailing lists that relate to that particular topic. Clicking on an individual list gives you a description and contact information about the list.

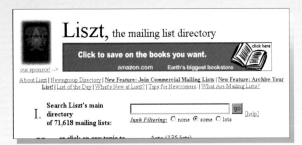

2 To search for a mailing list on Liszt, type a word or phrase to describe the type of mailing list you're looking for, and then press Enter.

3 After a while, Liszt displays the mailing lists whose names or descriptions contain the search text. Click on a list to get detailed subscription information.

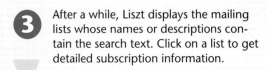

4 Liszt displays the list and administrative addresses for the list, as well as thorough subscription instructions.

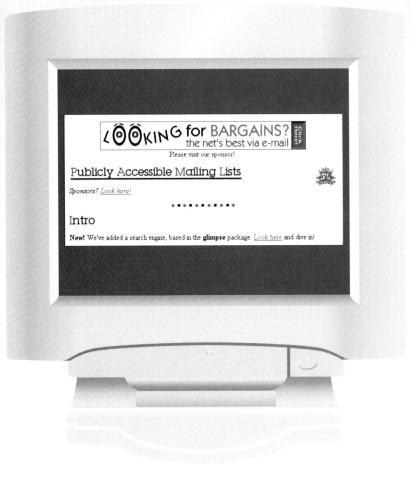

5 Publicly Accessible Mailing Lists (shown in the middle of the page) is another well-known list of mailing lists. To reach it, punch up **http://www.neosoft.com/internet/paml**. As its name implies, this list includes only public mailing lists, and it provides complete information on each list.

6 Click on Index to search an index of lists.

How to Subscribe to a Mailing List

Most mailing lists use software programs to process subscription requests automatically. The most widely used program is Listserv. Two other commonly used list-management programs are Majordomo and Listproc. Although the techniques for subscribing (and unsubscribing) are similar for all automated lists, the syntax of the commands varies, so read the subscription instructions carefully.

1 Every mailing list has two e-mail addresses with completely different purposes: The *List address* is where you send e-mail to contribute to the actual discussion; mail you send to the list address is distributed to all the subscribers. The *Administrative address* is where you send e-mail to subscribe, unsubscribe, get help, or customize the way the list works.

8 To unsubscribe from a mailing list, send a message to the administrative address. Leave the subject line blank, and type the command *signoff listname* in the message area. You'll receive a brief message stating that your request was received, and within the next day or so, you'll receive confirmation that you've been removed from the list.

● **Create a separate mail folder for each mailing list you join, and save the confirmation and welcome messages in these folders. This will make it easy to locate the unsubscribe commands.**

● **Many lists allow you to reduce the sheer number of e-mail messages by sending a command to the administrative address requesting that messages get sent to you in *digest* form. This option tells the list-management software to consolidate the messages into batches instead of sending them to you individually.**

```
Welcome to the twilight2000 mailing list!

Please save this message for future reference.  Thank you.

If you ever want to remove yourself from this mailing list,
you can send mail to <Majordomo@lists.MPGN.COM> with the following
command in the body of your email message:

    unsubscribe twilight2000 mwalker@mail.neocomm.net

If you ever need to get in contact with the owner of the list,
(if you have trouble unsubscribing, or have questions about the
list itself) send email to <owner-twilight2000@lists.MPGN.COM> .
```

7 The Listserv software sends you a confirmation when you've been added to the list. Keep this message, since it gives you the list address, tells you how to unsubscribe, and explains how to customize the way the list works. (You might also receive a welcome message from the list administrator telling you more about the "culture" of the list and describing guidelines for maintaining a positive atmosphere in the discussion.)

2 To subscribe to a list, first display Netscape Mail's Message Composition window, and then type the administrative address in the Mail To text box. Leave the Subject text box blank (unless instructed to do otherwise).

```
Subject: subscribe twilight 2000
   Date: Thu, 10 Jul 1997 10:58:36 -0400
   From: "Mark H. Walker" <mwalker@neocomm.net>
Organization: Walker Publishing
     To: Majordomo@lists.MPGN.COM

subscribe twilight2000
```

3 Type the list subscription command in the text area. In this example, I typed the command **subscribe Twilight 2000** to subscribe to a mailing list about Twilight 2000, a futuristic role-playing game. (Mailing-list names are often displayed in uppercase, but the commands are not actually case sensitive.) Send the subscription request, and click on OK when Netscape asks if you want to send a message with no subject.

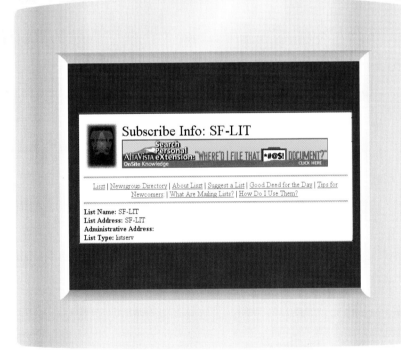

```
Subject: Majordomo results: subscribe twilight 2000
   Date: Thu, 10 Jul 1997 11:08:59 -0400
   From: Majordomo@Phaser.ShowCase.MPGN.COM
     To: mwalker@mail.neocomm.net

--

>>>> subscribe twilight2000
Succeeded.
```

4 You may receive an automated message asking that you confirm your identity by replying to the message with the word OK. On the other hand, many lists simply reply that your subscription request has succeeded (that is, has been received by the list software).

5 Next, a message informs you that your request has been forwarded to the list owner. You're not in the club yet; this message just lets you know that your request is being processed.

6 If the list is private, the list administrator may request more information, such as your reasons for wanting to join the list. Within a week or two of your reply, you'll receive a confirmation such as the one shown in step 7.

What Are Newsgroups?

For many years, people have been exchanging ideas, advice, and information in online discussion groups called newsgroups. There are thousands of newsgroups, each focusing on a particular topic. They are part of an Internet facility called Usenet and are distributed by machines called news servers.

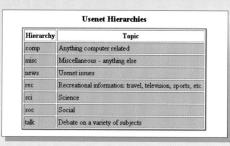

Usenet Hierarchies

Hierarchy	Topic
comp	Anything computer related
misc	Miscellaneous – anything else
news	Usenet issues
rec	Recreational information: travel, television, sports, etc.
sci	Science
soc	Social
talk	Debate on a variety of subjects

1 Newsgroups are organized hierarchically, which makes them easier to find. Some of the major hierarchies are *comp* (computers), *sci* (science), *rec* (recreation), *soc* (social issues), and *news* (newsgroup-related topics).

5 Before experimenting with newsgroups, make sure you have told Netscape Navigator the name of your ISP's news server. (Choose Options, Mail and News Preferences, click on the Servers tab, and type the name in the News (NNTP) Server text box.)

2 Each hierarchy is divided into branches and possibly subbranches. A newsgroup's name indicates where it fits in a particular hierarchy. For example, the rec.animals.wildlife newsgroup is in the animals branch of the rec hierarchy.

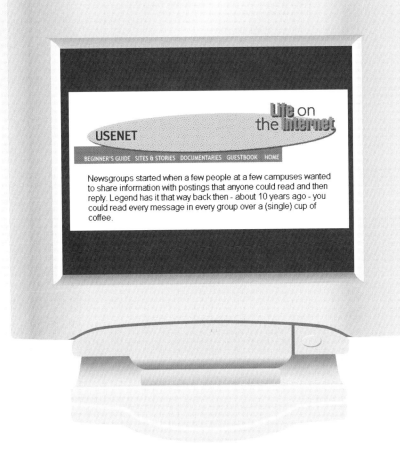

3 You'll need a *newsreader* to access newsgroups. The newsreader described in the next few pages is Netscape News, which is integrated into Netscape Navigator. However, you can check out shareware newsreaders, such as Free Agent (available at **http://www.tucows.com**).

4 Internet Explorer also has a top-notch newsreader—Internet News.

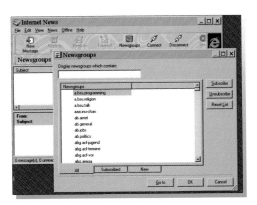

How to Search Newsgroups with Deja News

Finding newsgroups that interest you is important but not always easy. One company on the Web that addresses this problem is Deja News. It provides a fast and easy-to-use service that searches across all newsgroups for messages matching the criteria you specify.

1 In the main Netscape Navigator window, type the URL **http://dejanews.com** in the Location text box and press Enter to jump to the Deja News Web site.

8 To perform a more specialized search, click on the Power Search button at the top of Deja News' home page This button lets you specify whether Deja News should look for newsgroups messages that contain all the words you enter as your Search Criteria, or any of the words. You can also limit your search by newsgroup, date, or author. To get help on using Deja News, click on the Help Index button.

- To learn about searching for other resources on the Internet, refer to Part 4.

- If a message you posted to a newsgroup turns up in someone's search results, they can display your author profile (see step 7) to see a list of all the newsgroups to which you've recently posted messages.

7 Deja News displays an author profile, which includes a list of all the newsgroups to which the author has posted messages in the last month.

2 Enter your search criteria in the Quick Search For text box.

3 After a moment, Deja News displays the results of the search (also called a *hit list*) with the messages that most closely match your criteria listed at top. For each message, Deja News lists the date, the subject line, the newsgroup containing the message, and the name of the author.

4 If you see a newsgroup that looks interesting, jot it down. Follow the guidelines given in the next topic to subscribe to the newsgroup.

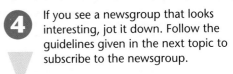
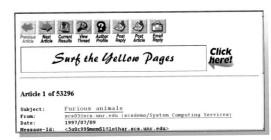

5 To read a message, click on the subject. Deja News displays the message. (In this example, only the message header information is visible without scrolling.) You can use the buttons at the top of the window to read other messages in the hit list, to post a message to the newsgroup, to send e-mail to the author, and so on.

6 If you want to find out more about a message's author, click on their name in the search results.

How to Subscribe to a Newsgroup

You've searched the Internet for a few newsgroups that interest you. Now you're ready to join the discussion. All you need to do is subscribe—that is, tell your newsreader which newsgroups to list for you. Here's how.

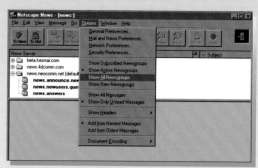

1 Choose Window, Netscape News to display the Netscape News window. The top-left pane lists the newsgroups carried by your ISP, the top-right pane lists messages within the selected newsgroup, and the bottom pane displays the contents of the selected message.

7 After you've subscribed to the newsgroups that interest you, choose Options, Show Subscribed Newsgroups to hide all newsgroups but the ones you've subscribed to, or choose Options, Show Active Newsgroups to see only subscribed newsgroups that contain new messages.

● To unsubscribe to a newsgroup, just clear its check box.

● The Options, Show New Newsgroups command shows only newsgroups that are new since you last connected to your news server.

● You can resize the three panes in the Netscape News window by dragging their gray borders.

2 Netscape News automatically subscribes you to three newsgroups that contain helpful information and advice for new users. The check marks next to the newsgroup names indicate your subscription. If you don't see any newsgroups, click on the plus sign next to the default news host to expand the display.

3 To find additional newsgroups to subscribe to, choose Options, Show All Newsgroups.

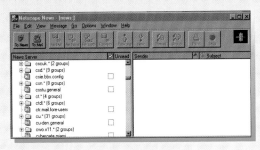

4 All the newsgroup hierarchies eventually appear in the newsgroup pane. (This can take several minutes.) The yellow folder icons represent newsgroup hierarchies (or branches within hierarchies). The page icons represent actual newsgroups.

5 As you scroll through the list, you'll see folders for all the main hierarchies (comp, news, rec, and so on), as well as for many others. Netscape lists the number of newsgroups in each hierarchy to the right of the hierarchy name. Click on the plus sign to the left of a hierarchy to expand it, displaying all the newsgroups and branches that hierarchy contains (and then click on the minus sign to collapse the view).

6 Each hierarchy contains some combination of newsgroups and folders (representing branches within the main hierarchy). Continue clicking on the folders until you find a newsgroup that catches your fancy. To subscribe, mark its check box. (Before deciding whether to subscribe to a newsgroup, you'll probably want to read a few of its messages. See the next topic.)

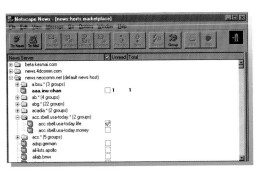

How to Read Newsgroup Messages

Newsgroup messages are similar to e-mail. Most readers, however, don't automatically save newsgroup messages on your computer. Instead, you view them in newsgroups stored on your ISP's news server. Each time you select a message, Netscape News transfers the information from the server to your computer, so newsgroup messages take longer to display than e-mail on your hard drive.

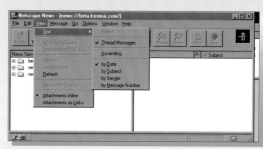

1 Choose Window, Netscape News to display the Netscape News window, and then select the desired newsgroup. You'll see the messages in the message header pane. Netscape News automatically *threads* newsgroup messages, organizing all the replies to one message in one branch. This makes it easier to follow the various discussions. (If this feature is off, you can turn it back on by choosing View, Sort, Thread Messages.)

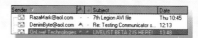

8 Click in the column to the right of the author name in the message header pane to flag messages. Once you flag messages, you can use the First Flagged, Next Flagged, and Previous Flagged commands in the Go menu to jump quickly between them.

7 Use the Thread button to mark entire threads as read, and the Group button to mark entire newsgroups as read. Assuming the Options, Show Only Unread Messages command is turned on, it's helpful to mark threads you're not interested in as read, so that the newsreader won't display them in the future.

6 To jump to the next, or previous, new message, click on the Next and Previous buttons in the toolbar.

● **To save a message to disk, select the message, choose File, Save As, type a name for the file in the File Name box, and click Save. Netscape News saves the message as a plain text file. Save messages that you're interested in, since old messages are deleted from newsgroups at regular intervals.**

● **To print a message, select the message, click on the Print toolbar button, and then click OK.**

● **Newsgroup messages can contain attached documents or URLs. Handle these attachments the same way you did e-mail attachments.**

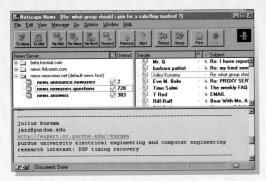

2 Netscape News boldfaces new messages and marks them with the green Unread flag. To read a message, click on it. Netscape News clears the Unread flag and displays the contents of the message in the message text pane. The message begins with the subject and the date, and then lists information about the author and the newsgroups to which the author posted the message. The References line contains links to any previous messages in the current thread.

3 Some newsgroups are moderated, meaning that all incoming messages are reviewed to determine whether they are inappropriate, offensive, or unrelated to the newsgroup. The quality of the discussion in moderated groups is often better than that of unmoderated groups. To discover if a newsgroup is moderated, first choose Options, Show Headers, All to list more detailed information at the beginning of each message.

4 Moderated newsgroups have a line called Approved at the beginning of each message, listing the names of the people who moderate the group. (To hide this detailed information, choose Options, Show Header, Normal.)

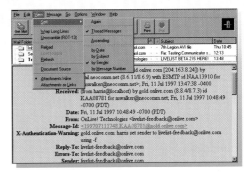

5 To change the order in which Netscape lists newsgroup messages, choose one of the four options at the bottom of the View, Sort submenu. The default sort option is By Date; this lists the most recent messages at the top. By Subject and By Author arrange messages alphabetically by subject or author, and By Message Number sorts messages by the order of arrival at the news server.

How to Interact with Newsgroups

If you'd like to participate in a newsgroup, but you aren't sure what the ground rules are, these suggestions will help you feel comfortable joining a discussion. A word of warning: Newsgroups are a forum for everyone. As in the real (noncyber world), you'll meet some people who are polite and responsible, and others who are rude and thoughtless. Be nice to the former, flame the later, and move on.

1 When you find a newsgroup that interests you, browse the messages before posting your own. This way, you avoid asking previously posted questions, and you can get a feel for the culture of the group.

8 Don't sweat it! Yeah, these seem like a lot of rules. Don't worry, you don't have to memorize them. Just treat people in newsgroups with the same respect you would in a face to face encounter and you'll do fine.

- In addition to smileys, many newsgroup messages include abbreviations such as BTW (by the way), IMHO (in my humble opinion), FWIW (for what it's worth), and <g> (grin).

- More sophisticated newsreaders have kill commands that let you screen out certain messages based on keywords, subjects, threads, and authors. This makes it easier to ignore obnoxious messages.

7 Read FAQs whenever you find them. FAQs (Frequently Asked Questions) are lists of answers to common questions. Many newsgroups regularly post FAQs for newcomers, and newsgroups ending with *.answers* contain only FAQs. The three newsgroups that Netscape News automatically subscribes you to (news.announce.newusers, news.newusers.questions, and news.answers) contain FAQs on everything you need to know about participating in newsgroups.

2 If you disagree with most of the postings, it's better to unsubscribe from the group than to write numerous messages criticizing what you see. Newsgroups really are somewhere that you can't fight city hall (that is, the prevailing attitude).

3 Uppercased words are interpreted as shouting—don't do it. Unless, of course, you are speaking with someone who doesn't understand English. Then, it is perfectly acceptable to type slowly and use all caps. (Just kidding.)

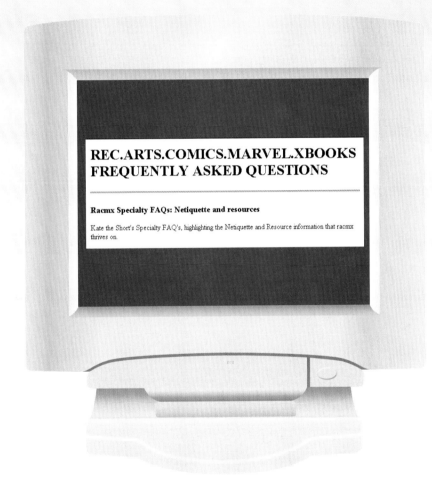

REC.ARTS.COMICS.MARVEL.XBOOKS FREQUENTLY ASKED QUESTIONS

Racmx Specialty FAQs: Netiquette and resources

Kate the Short's Specialty FAQ's, highlighting the Netiquette and Resource information that racmx thrives on.

4 If you want to add a bit of humor (as I attempted in the previous paragraph), you can use a smiley to make sure people understand that you're joking. A *smiley* is a sequence of characters that, when viewed sideways, looks like a facial expression. Some examples are :-) to express a smile, ;-) to show a wink, and :-(to express sadness.

6 Don't post inappropriate messages. Irrelevant messages dilute a newsgroup's quality and often anger other readers. Similarly, unless the newsgroup was designed for commerce, posting messages to sell a service or product is, as Peter Pan would say, "Bad Form."

5 Keep your messages brief, and use meaningful subject lines. For example, the subject "How do I modify my Lola T-342's suspension?" is more meaningful than "Help!" If you're asking for help, supply enough information so that people can give you the assistance you need.

How to Post a Newsgroup Message

As the saying goes, "Life is not a spectator sport," and neither are newsgroups. Reading the posts is interesting, even amusing, but sooner or later you're going to want to throw in your own opinions.

These steps explain how to post or reply to a message. (Before posting, you should read "How to Interact with Newsgroups" to learn basic newsgroup etiquette.)

1 Posting a new message in a newsgroup starts a new thread. In contrast, replying to a message adds your message to an existing thread.

- You can type a URL directly into the body of a message. In the posted message, it will appear as a hypertext link.

- While short quotes from an original message can make your reply more understandable, be careful to avoid including unnecessarily large sections of original text. This can make your messages long and boring.

- When you're replying to a message, check the Newsgroups text box and delete any newsgroups you don't want to send your response to.

5 To reply to a message, first click on the message. Next, click on one of three buttons in the toolbar: Re: Mail, Re: News, or Re: Both. (The Re: Mail button sends your reply, via private e-mail, to the original message's author. Re: News post's your reply in the newsgroup. Re: Both does both.) Type your response and send it.

2 Choose Window, Netscape News, and click on the newsgroup to which you want to post a message. Next, click on the To:News toolbar button (or choose File, New News Message).

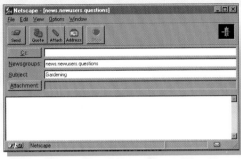

3 Netscape News opens the Message Composition window. The newsgroup name appears in the title bar and Newsgroups text box. To post your message to additional newsgroups, add their names to the Newsgroups text box, separating them with commas. To send the missive as an e-mail message as well, enter the e-mail address in the CC text box.

4 Enter a subject for the message in the Subject text box, type the message, and click Send.

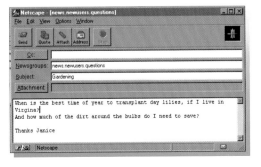

How to Chat with IRC

IRC, or Internet Relay Chat, is a popular way for people to "chat" on the Internet. Users may connect in specific chat areas, called channels, and participate in live discussions by typing on their keyboards.

1 The Internet Relay Chat FAQ Web site is a good place to start. Type the following URL into your browser and press Enter: **http://www. irchelp.org/**. The information at the top of the page is an excellent summary of what IRC is and how it works.

8 You can leave the current channel by closing the window. You can also open an additional channel by selecting it from the Channels folder. In fact, you can have multiple channels open at the same time, and you can switch between them as often as you like.

● Netscape users can download a special chat program called IChat. It is designed to work with the Netscape Navigator Web browser. You can download it for free from Netscape's home page at http://home.netscape.com.

7 And Viola! You're in an IRC session. The main chat window is divided into two panes. The left side of the window displays all the messages left by users on the channel. The right side of the window maintains a running list of all the participants in the channel. You can type a message and press Enter to broadcast it.

2 The IRC client application is the most crucial piece of the IRC puzzle. This software connects to IRC servers, enabling you to participate in an IRC session.

Welcome to the mIRC Homepage

United Kingdom, California, Utah, Washington, The Netherlands, Kuwait, Brazil, South Africa.
(please set a bookmark to the mirror site fastest for you)

mIRC's new **version 5.02** available worldwide.

IRC, short for Internet Relay Chat, offers a world-wide multi-user chat network, where people meet to talk in groups, or privately. Lots of people can participate in the real time discussions, and the number of topics covered on IRC is endless. On IRC you'll meet people with the same ideas and interests, and making friends for life is not unusual. IRC can host your business meetings and it can be your virtual hide-out!
To connect to IRC you'll need a small chat program like mIRC. mIRC is the shareware IRC chat program made for Windows by Khaled Mardam-Bey. It offers a fast and clean interface to IRC and it is well equipped with options and tools. You can download mIRC for free!

3 mIRC, a freeware program for Windows, is one of the most popular IRC client applications. You can download the latest version from the mIRC home page at **http://www.mirc.com**.

4 After downloading and installing mIRC, launch the program. After the application is running, you'll need to enter your setup information. Choose Setup from the File menu, or press Ctrl+E.

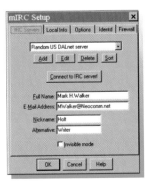

5 In the mIRC setup screen, choose a server from the server list. Then type in your real name and your e-mail address in the text entry boxes provided. You must also provide a nickname, which will be used to identify you on the IRC channels. You should also enter an alternate nickname, in case your first choice is already in use. Click the Connect button to log on to the IRC server.

6 Click on the channels folder on the mIRC toolbar to bring up a list of available channels. For starters, join a new users channel, such as #newbies. Click on either the Join or OK button once you have selected a channel.

How to Use the Proper Chat Etiquette

IRC has its own culture and rules of etiquette, often referred to as "netiquette." To avoid getting "flamed," or assaulted by e-mail for breaching the accepted rules of IRC, take a few minutes to read through the IRC FAQ and the following guidelines. Both will answer most of the basic questions you'll have about IRC.

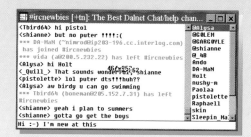

 Be nice. This is perhaps the cardinal rule. Don't type comments you wouldn't want others to type to you. To retread a well-worn path, "Type unto others as you would have them type unto you."

 Use a lot of smileys. When in doubt, put a smiley or <g> at the end of a sentence. Without visual cues, it's easy to misinterpret a message's meaning. You can, however, salve many a potential hurt feeling with a simple <g> (grin) at the end of your communication.

2 Be patient. Don't expect an immediate answer to each comment you type. Those electrons take a while to travel back and forth. So, before you SHOUT (type in all caps) at someone to pay attention, give them a couple of minutes.

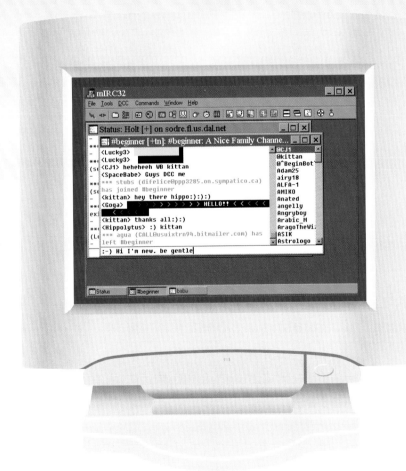

3 Don't shout. Using all caps is considered shouting, just as it is when typing newsgroup messages.

 4 Be brief. The server has to process each word you type. More is not better.

How to Use Voice-Aided Chat

First there were newsgroups, then IRC, now voice chat. Will the fun never stop? The latest advance in Web socializing, voice chat is similar to Internet telephony, but it enables multiple users to gather at one place (that is, one server) and shoot the breeze.

Netsite: http://www.onlive.com/

1 A popular voice chat application is OnLive! Traveler. Their Web address is **http://www.onlive.com**.

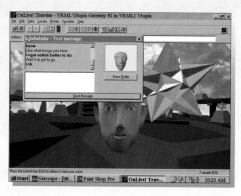

8 If you have chosen a VMRL site, you may negotiate through the site using your keyboard's arrow keys.

7 Subsequently, OnLive! Traveler will connect you to your chosen site. Once there, you may speak by pressing Crtl. Use the toolbar at the top of the screen to change the expression of your avatar, locate other netizens at the site, or obtain a site map.

FYI

● Right-clicking on another avatar's head will pop up a list of options, including sending text messages. Just type your message and send it. This is a nice feature when your connection is not good enough for voice transmissions.

● In a VMRL site, you may move your avatar up and down by pressing the Alt key as you press the keyboard's forward and backward arrow.

2 Once you have reached their Web site, download the latest version of OnLive! Traveler. Once downloaded, install the software and restart your computer. Pay special attention to the application's hardware requirements, such as microphone and 16-bit sound application.

3 Double-click on the OnLive icon to start the program. This will also run your browser and dialer to hook you up to your ISP.

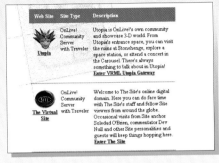

4 You'll land on OnLive's chat site page. OnLive offers some fascinating online communities, from a Monday Night Football club to MTV Tikkiland. Click on the one you wish to visit.

6 The first time you use OnLive! Traveler, it will help you set up and test your microphone. Merely follow the on-screen prompts.

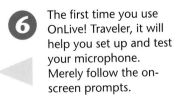

5 Next, you'll be prompted to create an *avatar*, or on-screen personage. There are several to choose from. Additionally you can even modify the facial expression (sad, happy, angry, neutral).

How to Game on the Internet

The number of online gamers has ballooned in the last couple of years. In early 1996, commercial online gaming sites were no more than a "Gee, wouldn't it be great" idea. Today, hundreds of thousands of gamers play online each month. Here is a sample of places you can meet them.

1 Mplayer is probably the largest online gaming site, at least in terms of online participants. They offer a healthy selection of games (including Quake, Command and Conquer, and so on), voice chat in the game room lobbies, tournaments, and more. The address for the Mplayer home page is **http://www.mplayer.com**. You can sign up there.

5 All the online services, such as AOL, MSN, CompuServe, Prodigy, and Genie offer some form of on-line gaming. Check each for its own gaming information.

● Be advised, none of these sites are free—although Mplayer is dirt cheap. You can expect, at least for the moment, to pay to play. Most of these sites, however, offer a free trial period.

● Online time can be expensive. If you plan to spend some serious Internet game time, you'd best sign up for your ISP's unlimited service plan.

2 The Total Entertainment Network (TEN) was one of the first online game sites. They don't dish out quite as many games as Mplayer, nor do they offer voice chatting, but their clientele is a wee bit...shall we say, more mature? Turn your browser to **http://www.ten.net** to find this site.

3 2AM Games is a newer and smaller gaming site. Its developers believe the heart of online games is interaction, not do-or-die competition. You won't find Duke Nukem 3D or Warcraft 2 here. Although 2AM games have winners and losers, the developers have designed them to get teams of players working together. You can find this interaction at **http://www.2am.com**.

4 Just as new as 2AM, but on the other end of the size spectrum, is Game Gateway. Kind of a gaming supersite, Game Gateway has combined the services of several on-line game sites at one location. They have a large selection of games and promise many more. They can be found at **http://www.gamegateway.com**.

Joining an Online Game Service

Joining a online game service is easy. All of them offer the downloadable software at their site. Download the software, install it, log on, and sign in. Read on and we'll walk you through the process with Mplayer.

1 Head over to the Mplayer Web site. Hopefully, it will be where we left it a page ago (http://www.mplayer.com).

8 Once the game is downloaded, you'll be able to enter a game room and play the game.

● Voice chat is enabled only inside Mplayer game rooms.

● You may not play in "Red" game rooms. Your ISP connection is not fast enough to support that level of game play.

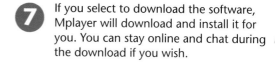

7 If you select to download the software, Mplayer will download and install it for you. You can stay online and chat during the download if you wish.

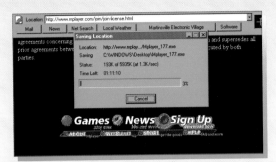

2 Download the basic Mplayer software by clicking on Sign Up. Don't worry about selecting any games.

3 Install Mplayer by double-clicking on the previously downloaded Mplayer file. After installation is complete, Mplayer will plop a M player icon on your desktop (this may be in the Mplayer folder).

4 Connect to your ISP (using your dial-up application) and double-click on the Mplayer icon.

5 Mplayer will throw you into their main lobby. From here you can choose which game to play. Double-clicking on the game's icon will take you to the specific game lobby. If the game is marked with an *R*, you need a retail (store bought) version to play the game.

6 If you need to download the game software (this will be the case if you've never played), Mplayer will prompt you to do so. Even if the game you wish to play requires retail software that you own, you'll need the Mplayer enabling software.

How to Use MUDs

MUDs (multiuser dungeons) are another, albeit dated, form of Internet gaming. MUDs can be addictive, and it's easy to get trapped inside. A MUD is an interactive game in which you assume the identity of a character and play against other online characters. MUDs come in many different shapes and sizes, but all of them share one thing: They're a lot of fun. This section will point you to some MUD resources and show you how to get started in the world of MUDs.

1 MUDs are not actually part of the World Wide Web. They are accessed through a Telnet connection using a Telnet client application. While any Telnet application will do, using a specialized MUD client program is an even better choice. A good place to start your search for a MUD client is the Winsock Game Clients page at **http://www.rahul.net/galen/client.html**. This page contains information and links to many popular MUD programs, and even has a chart comparing their features.

● *MUD* is often used as a catch-all term for any role-playing game on the Internet, but there are lots of different varieties. Object-oriented MUDs are called MOOs, and MUSHs are multiuser shared hallucinations.

2 One of the best MUD client programs is Zugg's MUD Client (zMUD), which you can download from the zMUD home page at **http://www.zuggsoft.com**. This full-featured MUD client boasts a Connection Wizard that makes accessing MUDs a snap.

3 Once you've downloaded and installed your MUD client, you need to find a MUD game to join. Most client programs come with a list of available MUDs, but you can find a current and comprehensive list on the Web at the Mud Connector Web page. The URL is **http://www.mudconnect.com/ mud_category.html**.

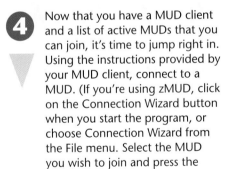

4 Now that you have a MUD client and a list of active MUDs that you can join, it's time to jump right in. Using the instructions provided by your MUD client, connect to a MUD. (If you're using zMUD, click on the Connection Wizard button when you start the program, or choose Connection Wizard from the File menu. Select the MUD you wish to join and press the Connect button.)

5 Once you're connected to a MUD, follow the directions on the screen carefully. Getting used to the world of MUDs takes a little time. It's a good idea to type *help* at the prompt to get specific information on commands you can use in the MUD. For general help with MUDs, you can access the MUD Resource Collection page at **http://www.cis.upenn.edu/~lwl/ mudinfo.html**.

P A R T 8

New Technologies and Software

INTERNET TECHNOLOGY is advancing by leaps and bounds. What were cutting-edge applications a year ago are now taken for granted. In this section, we'll take a look at some of the newest software available to make using the Internet faster, more fun, and more productive.

Perhaps one of the more significant developments has been the introduction, albeit in beta form, of Netscape's and Microsoft's "next generation" browsers: Netscape Communicator and Microsoft Internet Explorer 4.0. Because of their importance, we'll spend a lot of ink discussing them; however, we'll also show you some of the other recent developments in Internet software.

IN THIS SECTION YOU'LL LEARN

- How to Download Netscape Communicator — 182
- How to Install Communicator — 184
- How to Configure Communicator — 186
- How to E-Mail with Communicator — 188
- How to Access Newsgroups with Communicator — 190
- How to Use Other Communicator Features — 192
- How to Download Internet Explorer 4.0 — 194
- How to Install Internet Explorer 4.0 — 196
- How to Use IE's Shell Integration — 198
- How to Use IE's Active Desktop — 200
- How to Configure Internet Explorer 4.0 — 202
- Browsing Offline with Internet Explorer — 204
- How to E-Mail with Internet Explorer 4.0 — 206
- How to Access Newsgroups with IE4 — 208
- How to Post to Newsgroups Using IE4 — 210
- How to Use Other IE4 Features — 212
- A Look at Web TV — 214
- How to Download and Install CU-SeeMe — 216
- How to Use CU-SeeMe — 218
- How to Download and Install Voice E-Mail — 220
- How to Use Voice E-Mail — 222

How to Download Netscape Communicator

Netscape Communicator is the latest version of the popular Navigator browser. Although the interface will be familiar to Navigator veterans, there are some changes and several new additions.

1 Cruise over to the Netscape site located at http://home.netscape.com, or, if you are using Navigator, click the Netscape button.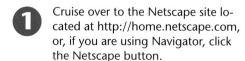

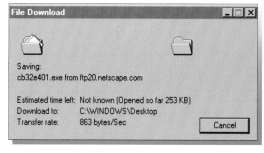

5 The download should take about 50 minutes with a 28.8-kbps modem and a decent connection.

● You can continue to work on your computer as you download. It will, however, slow the transfer rate.

● Check out the other add-ons while you're at the Netscape site. Click on the Download Software button at the bottom of the page for more information.

2 Head to the Communicator download site. Netscape, like most large companies, is constantly updating its Web site. Although you may currently link to the download site by clicking "Tune up to Communicator," the link may change before publication. Just look for the hypertext download link.

3 Choose whether you want to buy the software (including software support) or download a trial version for free.

4 As we have discussed previously, the Desktop is the best place to direct your downloads. If you do, there is no chance of forgetting where they are.

How to Install Communicator

O f course downloading Communicator is only half the battle. Now you must fight the installation wars.

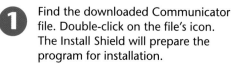

1 Find the downloaded Communicator file. Double-click on the file's icon. The Install Shield will prepare the program for installation.

● There are numerous download sites for Communicator. If the Netscape site is congested, click on the Other Sites link on Netscape's home page.

● Netscape "subscribers" (those that have bought the software) are allowed access to a special high-speed, low-drag download site, which speeds their downloads.

2 Remember, during installation you must exit all other Windows programs. If you don't, you're asking for trouble.

3 Note that Communicator doesn't replace, write over, or uninstall previous versions of Navigator present on your computer. If you wish to do so, you must use the Add/Remove programs option under the Control Panel.

4 When completed, Communicator will drop a new Communicator window on your screen. Composer, Collabra, Messenger, and Navigator—the different applications within Communicator—are included in the window.

How to Configure Communicator

The final step in converting to Communicator is configuring your new software. The following pages will show you what to do and some of the pitfalls to avoid.

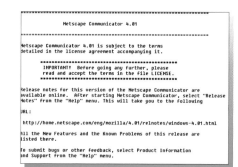

Before configuring Communicator, be sure to read the Readme file. It contains setup tips and other useful information.

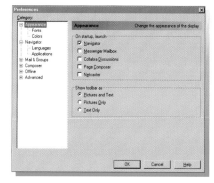

You can also choose which Communicator modules run when the program starts. To do so, select Appearance, instead of Navigator, and put a check mark in the boxes beside the software you want to run.

● There isn't enough room to cover all of Communicator's configuration options. However, most can be set under the Edit/Preferences menu.

● Cookies, did someone mention cookies? Communicator gives you multiple options for dealing with cookies. Select the Advanced options under the Edit/Preferences drop-down menu.

2 The first time you click on the spanking new Communicator icon, Netscape will offer several choices for configuring the system. For instance, you may set up Communicator to handle different users, each with their own e-mail address and password.

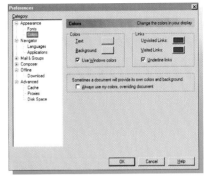

3 Once the Communicator browser screen fills the window, click on Edit, then Preferences. Here you can change most anything in the browser to suite your preferences.

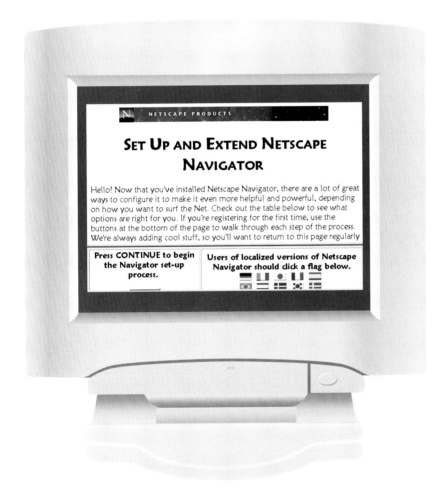

4 To reset the startup page, pull down the Edit menu, choose Preferences, and select Navigator. Click in the circle beside Home Page and type in the desired URL in the location box.

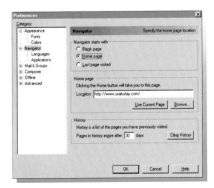

How to E-Mail with Communicator

E-mailing with Communicator is easy. Messenger is Communicator's messaging application, and most of its functions will be familiar to veteran Netscapers.

1 To start Messenger, click on the Mailbox icon on the Communicator Component bar. The bar is located in the lower-right corner of your Navigator browser.

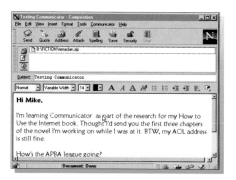

6 To attach a file, click the Attach icon. Click on File, select the file from the Look In box, and click Open. Notice that the Attach File and Document's paper clip turns red. You can review the attached files by clicking on the Attach File and Document's icon.

● Messenger will encrypt your message, but you must have a certificate (which includes their public encryption key) from each addressee. You can obtain a list of certificates you have either collected or owned by accessing Security and then Certificates and Signatures in the Communicator Help database. See Part 6 for more information.

● Communicator's messenger comes with a spell checking feature. To use it, punch the Spelling button on the Message toolbar.

2 You can also start Messenger by clicking on its icon, which is usually located in the Communicator folder, or by selecting Programs from the Start menu, then choosing Netscape Communicator, Messenger.

3 To open a new e-mail message, click the New Message icon on the Messenger toolbar.

4 Type the recipient's address or, if they are in your address book, tap the Address icon, pick the recipient, and select the To button.

5 Type the message text and hit Send.

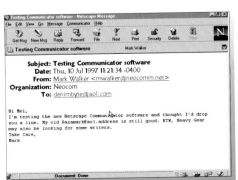

How to Access Newsgroups with Communicator

Most of Communicator's features will seem familiar to Navigator veterans. Netscape has, however, made significant changes to the newsreader interface, so follow along if you don't want to spend a lot of time hunting and pecking for the right menu.

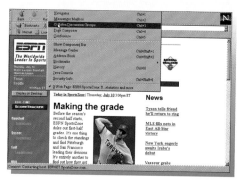

1 Communicator's newsreader is Collabra. Start the program either by clicking on its icon in the Component toolbar, selecting the Communicator pull-down menu and clicking on Collabra Discussion Groups, or choosing Programs from the Start menu, then picking Netscape Communicator, and finally Collabra.

7 You can unsubscribe to a newsgroup by clicking on your server and choosing Subscribe. Once Collabra displays the Subscribe to Discussion Groups window, you can highlight the group in question and tap Unsubscribe.

6 You can send your own message to the group by clicking Reply or New Msg in the toolbar. Reply answers the message you were viewing, and New Msg puts a totally new message in the newsgroup.

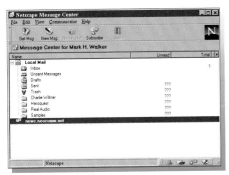

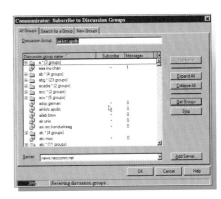

2 Collabra displays the Netscape Message Center shown here. To view the newsgroups to which your server subscribes, highlight the server and click Subscribe in the Toolbar.

3 Here are some of my server's newsgroups.

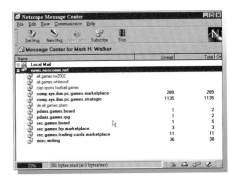

4 To subscribe to a newsgroup, select Subscribe while the newsgroup is highlighted, then hit OK. The Message Center opens with your newsgroups displayed under the server. These are some of the newsgroups I've subscribed to.

5 To read the messages under a header, double-click on the header.

How to Use Other Communicator Features

Communicator and Internet Explorer 4.0 are the wave of the future. The preceding pages, while plenty to get you up and running, merely skimmed the surface of Communicator's abilities. Now let's take a look at some of Communicator's other features.

1 Netscape Composer is a powerful online document authoring tool included in Communicator. Composer uses a What You See Is What You Get (WYSIWYG) editing tool.

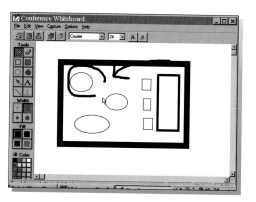

7 The whiteboard can be used between two people online to diagram ideas, convey graphical messages, and so on.

- In addition to the modules covered here, the Netscape Communicator Professional edition comes with advanced scheduling and LAN system administrator tools.

- There are tons of plug-ins for both Navigator and Communicator at the Netscape site. Check them out at http://home.netscape.com/comprod/server_add_ons.html/.

3 The WYSIWYG editor is a beautiful tool. Using, for the most part, what are familiar word processing commands, you can create top-notch Web pages or edit existing pages. To learn more, click Composer's Help menu.

2 To start Composer from the Communicator Navigator browser, pull down the File menu and select New. Next you must choose whether you want to open a blank page or use the Page Template or Page Wizard.

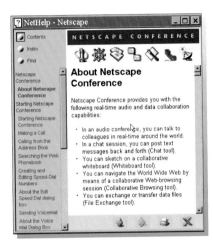

4 Communicator's Conference module allows you to converse—via audio, typed chat, or whiteboard—with similarly equipped people on the Internet.

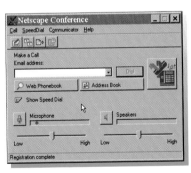

6 Once up and running, Conference looks like this sample screen. Clicking on the address book will take you to the 411 Internet White Pages. From this screen you can speak with people on the Internet, browse Web pages together, chat via keyboard input, and use the whiteboard.

5 To start Conference, double-click the Conference icon in the Communicator folder or pull down the Communicator menu and click on Conference.

How to Download Internet Explorer 4.0

Netscape's main competition in the browser wars is Microsoft's Internet Explorer. Internet Explorer 4.0 is Microsoft's answer to Netscape Communicator; it offers the same basic features and throws in a few interesting twists.

1 To download Internet Explorer 4.0, mosey over to the Microsoft home page (http://www.microsoft.com) and select Download 4.0.

FYI

● The Internet Explorer 4.0 beta preview includes a shell integration package that will change your Windows 95 interface. This can be unsettling to novice computer users. If you are not an experienced Windows 95 user, I don't recommend downloading the IE4 beta preview.

● Select the download site nearest you. This reduces the download time.

2 As we write this, Internet Explorer is merely a beta preview. The application is finicky, and the interface may change slightly. Microsoft does not recommend that workaday folks like ourselves use IE4 as our everyday browser. At least not yet.

3 As of this writing, you can download a standard, enhanced, or full version of the Microsoft Internet Explorer 4.0 beta. Each version comes with progressively more add-ons. Unfortunately, the more capable the version, the longer the download. The full version, for instance, is a 20MB file, which takes about four hours to download with a 28.8 modem.

4 Choose a download location, go to the next screen, and download the software.

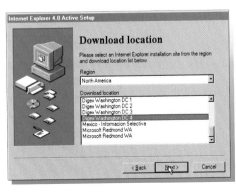

How to Install Internet Explorer 4.0

A t last, after the multi-hour download, the IE4 software waits expectantly on your hard drive. The good news is—it's an easy install. The bad news is—it takes 15–20 minutes.

1 Once downloaded, Internet Explorer automatically installs itself, with some input from you.

FYI

● If the computer does hang during installation, don't hit Ctrl+Alt+Del. Instead, Microsoft recommends that you turn off the computer, wait a minute, then turn it on. Find the folder where the downloaded IE4 installation file resides, double-click it, and try again.

● You can get installation help at the IE4 setup help page. It is located at http://www.microsoft.com/ie/ie40/download/support.htm.

2 IE4's installation routine will prompt you to close all applications, including your Internet connection. Pressing Alt+Tab will display the currently active applications. Shut them all down.

3 IE4 offers a default installation directory. You may use it or create your own by typing the directory over the current selection.

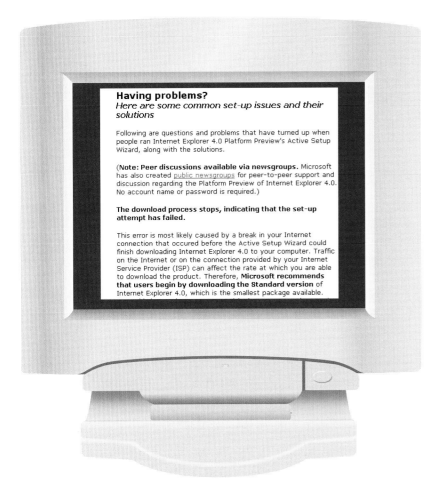

Having problems?
Here are some common set-up issues and their solutions

Following are questions and problems that have turned up when people ran Internet Explorer 4.0 Platform Preview's Active Setup Wizard, along with the solutions.

(**Note: Peer discussions available via newsgroups.** Microsoft has also created public newsgroups for peer-to-peer support and discussion regarding the Platform Preview of Internet Explorer 4.0. No account name or password is required.)

The download process stops, indicating that the set-up attempt has failed.

This error is most likely caused by a break in your Internet connection that occured before the Active Setup Wizard could finish downloading Internet Explorer 4.0 to your computer. Traffic on the Internet or on the connection provided by your Internet Service Provider (ISP) can affect the rate at which you are able to download the product. Therefore, **Microsoft recommends that users begin by downloading the Standard version** of Internet Explorer 4.0, which is the smallest package available.

4 IE4 will now install itself, providing the status of the installation as it goes.

5 Be patient. As we said, IE4 takes a while to install. There may be times when it appears to be doing nothing. Don't get trigger happy with the computer's On/Off switch. Stand up, get a cup of coffee, and come back.

How to Use IE's Shell Integration

The Internet Explorer 4.0 Platform Preview includes something called shell integration. During installation, IE4 reconfigures your Windows 95 interface to integrate the Internet more fully into your desktop. A great idea, but nevertheless, at first it can be a tad confusing.

1 Notice how "Explorerish" the new integrated desktop window looks. That's because it is! You can browse the Web from any of these windows.

● Shell integration does away with the dreaded double-click. The mouse cursor is hot, highlighting each object it passes over, and a single click will start any program on which the mouse rests.

● Certainly *the* prominent feature of shell integration is the Active Desktop. We'll have more to say about this feature on the following pages.

7 Select Do Not Use Shell Integration on the next screen and click OK. The computer will churn electrons for awhile, prompt you to close all programs, and remove shell integration.

2 You can enter a URL or select one from your list of favorites...

3 ...and you're surfing.

4 You don't need to enter the entire URL. Start with "www" and type the rest.

5 If you are not currently connected, Internet Explorer will display your dialer and, with your permission, connect to your ISP.

6 You can turn off the shell integration feature if you prefer not to use it. Click the Windows 95 Control Panel (notice the new, cursor-sensitive help, courtesy of IE4 shell integration), then select Add/Remove Programs. Highlight Microsoft Explorer 4.0 Shell Integration Mode and click Add/Remove.

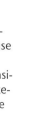

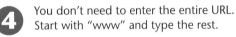

How to Use IE's Active Desktop

O ne of the snappiest features offered in IE's shell integration is the Active Desktop. Capable of simultaneously displaying several "windows to the Internet," Active Desktop is as useful as it is fun.

1 To change between the Active and "normal" Windows 95 desktops, right-click on the desktop screen and make your selection in the ensuing context menu.

8 Click Options, then Custom and set your preferences. Once finished, click OK and tell Explorer to download the object now. Here is a picture of my customized desktop.

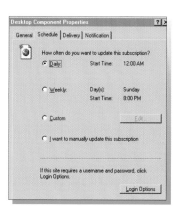

7 Explorer wants to know if you want the site updated daily. This is fine for graphical eye candy; however, news components will need to be updated more often.

● **Microsoft intends to post many more desktop components on their Web site. Drop by to see what they have.**

● **RAM is important when determining how many components you can put on your desktop without bogging down your computer. Obviously, the more RAM in your computer, the more active components it will run.**

2 The Active Desktop lets you add Active Desktop components. These components can be pictures, but most often you'll want to capture sections of or entire Web pages.

3 Clicking the "hey! i'm a desktop component" square will take you to Microsoft's Desktop Component Gallery (pictured in center). Here you can browse and subsequently choose a desktop component or two for your desktop.

4 These components, such as ESPN's, provide you with a constantly updated (at least as long as you are online) data link.

5 On the other hand, you may wish to add your own Active Desktop component. To do so, right-click on the desktop and select Properties.

6 On the Desktop page of the Display Properties dialog box, click New. Select whether you desire a Web site or picture. For this example we'll assume you're adding a Web site. Type in the URL of the site you wish to add and click OK.

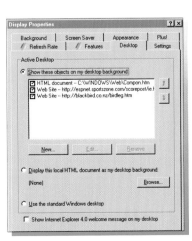

How to Configure Internet Explorer 4.0

S o far, we've discussed configuring the major options of Internet Explorer, such as the integrated shell and Active Desktop features. In this section we'll examine how to modify its everyday attributes to suit yourself.

1 To change the start page, head to your desired start page.

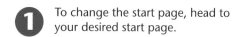

● You can also increase or decrease the size of the display text by choosing View, Fonts and then selecting the size you want.

● Additionally, Internet Explorer contains a Web-blocking routine. Consult Help for instructions on its use.

6 Next, on the General Tab of the Options dialog box, click Font Settings. In the Fixed Width and Proportional Font lists, choose the fonts you desire.

2 Once you arrive, select View, Options. In the Options dialog box, choose the Navigation tab, then click Use Current.

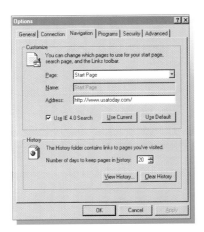

3 By now you probably have a favorite search page. Let's make it IE's default search tool: First, go to the Web page. Next, select View, Options.

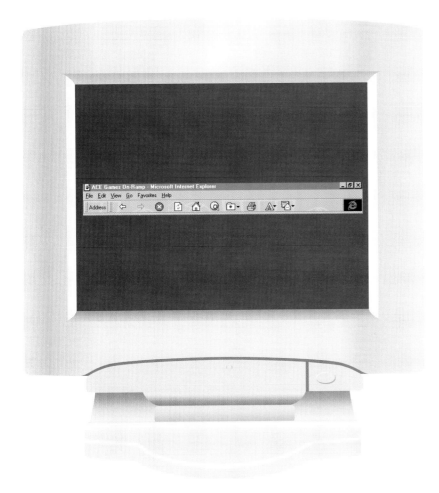

4 On the Navigator tab of the Options dialog box, choose Search Page from the Pages drop-down list. Tap Use Current.

5 You can also customize the fonts Internet Explorer 4.0 displays. First select View, Options.

Browsing Offline with Internet Explorer

Drumming your fingers while your favorite Web site boots byte by byte is no fun. Nevertheless, for one reason or another, that is frequently the case. Internet Explorer, however, will let you subscribe to sites, update them when it is convenient for you, and view them offline. No fuss, no muss.

1 To browse offline, you must first select, or subscribe to, the sites you wish to view.

6 To browse the Web offline, select File from any Internet Explorer window. (Remember, with IE's shell integration, any open folder is an Internet Explorer window.) Then click Browse Offline.

● Be careful when setting the delivery preferences. If you download two pages deep into a large Web site, you'll have a ton of information.

2 Go to the Web page you wish to subscribe to. Select Favorites, Add to Favorites. In the Add to Favorites dialog box, put a check mark in the Subscribe for Downloading box and click OK.

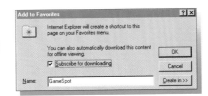

3 Next, you'll see the Subscription menu. Click Properties to set your parameters.

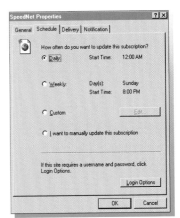

4 On the Schedule tab, schedule how often, and when, you want the page updated (for example, daily).

5 On the Delivery tab, you can set your delivery preferences. Likewise for the Notification tab.

How to E-Mail with Internet Explorer 4.0

Although similar to Microsoft Exchange and to the Navigator e-mail routines, IE4's Outlook Express has subtly altered the standard Microsoft e-mail interface. Here's a look at what IE4 has in store for you.

1 To open Outlook Express, click the package and letter icon on the Taskbar.

● You can organize your mail in folders. To do so, select File, Folder, New. Type in the name of your folder and hit Enter. Now you can drag and drop files into the folder.

● You can automatically record the address of the recipient of every e-mail you reply to in your address book. Select Tools, Mail Options. Click the appropriate box under the Read tab.

2 To send mail, click the New Message button in the toolbar. This opens a blank message on your screen.

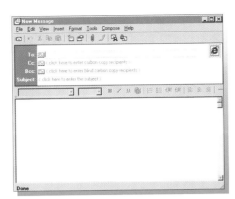

3 Fill in the usual suspects (address, CC, subject, and message text) and click the flying envelope icon to send your e-mail.

4 Unfortunately, this only places the mail in your outbox.

5 To send, click on the Send and Receive icon in Outlook Express toolbar or select Tools, Send and Receive. This will not only send mail in your outbox but also retrieve any mail on your mail server.

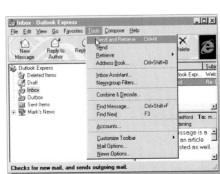

How to Access Newsgroups with IE4

Certainly no browser suite worth its code comes without newsgroup software. And Internet Explorer 4.0 is certainly worth its code. These pages explain how to use the newsgroup section of Outlook Express.

1 To browse newsgroups, from any browser window select Go, News.

8 Double-click on a message to see it full sized.

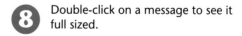

7 The messages will appear in the top-right pane. To read a message, click on it once or highlight it and press the space-bar. The message will fill the bottom-right, or Preview, pane.

FYI

● You can adjust the size of the separate panes in the Outlook Express Newsgroup window by dragging their borders.

● You can delete or compact your file database by choosing Clean Up from the Files pull-down menu.

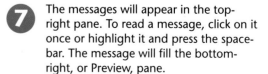

2 From the Outlook Express window, select Tools, Newsgroups. If you are not connected to your newsgroup server, connect.

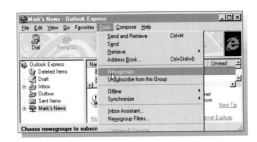

3 Usually, if you have already established a dial-up networking connection, you are hooked to your server. If you are connected, tell Outlook to try to find the server on the current connection.

4 Outlook Express will download the newsgroups your server carries.

5 To subscribe to a newsgroup, highlight the newsgroup from the All Newsgroups window. To unsubscribe, highlight a newsgroup from your subscribed newsgroups window and click Unsubscribe. After you are done subscribing/unsubscribing, click OK.

6 Now the newsgroups you have subscribed to will appear in the left-hand panel. To see a list of messages associated with a newsgroup, click on the newsgroup.

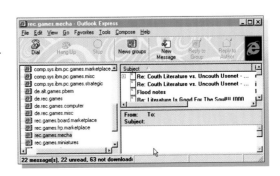

How to Post to Newsgroups Using IE4

Internet Explorer 4.0 offers a user-friendly interface for sending messages to newsgroups. Follow along and we'll take a look at it.

1 To post a new note to a newsgroup, click the New Message icon on the Outlook Express toolbar.

6 To reply to a newsgroup message, first double-click the message (just to bring it to full size). Next click on the appropriate reply icon: Reply to Group (sends to the entire newsgroup) or Reply to Author (sends it to anyone named Author—just kidding). Again, you may CC whomever you wish. Type in your message and click the Post It icon.

● You can check the spelling in any of your posts by pressing F7.

● You can send your post to any number of newsgroups. To do so, select Tools, Newsgroups, and add whichever newsgroups you want, following the same procedure you used in the address book.

2 A blank message form opens on your screen. The address of the news-group you were browsing is placed in the To line.

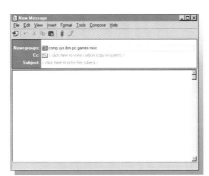

3 You can carbon copy individual recipients by entering their e-mail addresses on the CC line.

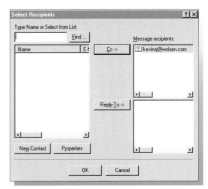

4 Clicking on the icon to the left of the CC line will open the ad-dress book. Once in the ad-dress book, highlight a name from the left panel and click CC (to carbon copy the person selected) or Reply-To (to send the message to the person).

5 Type your message and click the Post icon (at the top left of the message tool bar). If you wish to attach a file, click Insert File (the paper clip icon) and choose your file from the displayed Insert Attachment box.

How to Use Other IE4 Features

IE4 comes with a bucketload of new innovations and plug-ins (so does Netscape Communicator, for that matter). We don't have room to cover them all—it would take another book to do that—but here's a look at some of the salient features. Remember, at the risk of kicking a dead horse, that this book was written from the IE4 beta Platform Preview; some features may change before release.

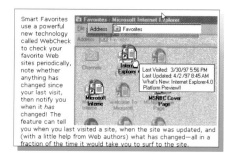

Smart Favorites use a powerful new technology called WebCheck to check your favorite Web sites periodically, note whether anything has changed since your last visit, then notify you when it *has* changed! The feature can tell you when you last visited a site, when the site was updated, and (with a little help from Web authors) what has changed—all in a fraction of the time it would take you to surf to the site.

1 With the Smart Favorites feature, IE can check on your favorite sites and let you know when the content has changed. However, you can't browse Smart Favorites offline.

FrontPad: Create your own Web pages!

Want to author your own Web pages? It's easy with FrontPad, one of the core components of Internet Explorer 4.0. FrontPad will take you step by step through the process of creating Web pages, plus it's a great tool for editing existing HTML documents. With FrontPad installed, the "Edit" button on the Internet Explorer 4.0 toolbar allows you to easily edit any page you view. Then you can use the Microsoft Web Publishing Wizard to post the modified page back to the server.

Microsoft FrontPad is a WYSIWYG (what-you-see-is-what-you-get) HTML editor based on Microsoft's award-winning and full-featured FrontPage 97 editor.

5 FrontPad is IE4's entry into the Web page design arena. Again, like Netscape's Composer, FrontPad is a WYSIWYG-type application and a snap to use.

- You can download the FrontPad and NetMeeting modules from the Microsoft site (http://www.microsoft.com).
- After you have designed that killer Web page with FrontPad, you can post it to your server using another application in IE4—Web Publishing Wizard.

2 To use Smart Favorites, from the Internet Explorer browser window click on Favorites, Subscriptions, Options. Under the General tab, check the Monitor Changes to My Favorite Web Sites option. You set the schedule in the same way as you do for offline subscriptions.

3 Whenever the content of one of your favorite Web sites changes, you'll see the red flash in its top-left corner when viewing your Favorites folder.

4 Another IE feature, NetMeeting is similar to Communicator's Conference in that it allows users to meet, talk, and chat online.

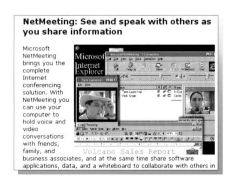

NetMeeting: See and speak with others as you share information

Microsoft NetMeeting brings you the complete Internet conferencing solution. With NetMeeting you can use your computer to hold voice and video conversations with friends, family, and business associates, and at the same time share software applications, data, and a whiteboard to collaborate with others in

A Look at WebTV

Is it a fad or is it here to stay? Is it a computer in TV's clothes or a TV masquerading as a Web browser? Who cares? It's a fun and unique way to surf the Web. On these pages we'll take a quick look at WebTV.

1 WebTV allows you to surf the Web, as well as send and receive e-mail from your TV. The technology is simple; in fact that is one of the medium's selling points.

● You must still pay Internet access fees when you use WebTV.

● There's no doubt that WebTV is easier, and cheaper, to use when surfing the Web, but you can't use it to do spreadsheets, write novels, or play any games that count. It is just a browser.

2 What makes WebTV work is its modem/adapter unit that connects your TV to an existing phone line.

3 Once turned on, the adapter/TV rig provides instant access to the World Wide Web. You can surf and send and reply to e-mail, just as you would from your PC.

4 You can control your browsing via a TV-type remote, keyboard, or remote infrared keyboard. You can switch between TV and WebTV with a click of the button.

6 WebTV has a number of advantages over PCs. For example, WebTV is simpler to set up and connect to the Internet, and it is much less expensive (less than $200 for a WebTV box) than a computer. In addition, WebTV provides a larger and more graphic Web experience.

5 Data is transmitted through a 33.6-kbps modem inside the WebTV box.

How to Download and Install CU-SeeMe

CU-SeeMe is video-conferencing software that lets you send video, audio, text, and graphics to similarly equipped users. Although the software is not free, you can download a free demo at the CU-SeeMe Web site.

1 Before you download, make sure your computer can run the software. You'll need the following: Windows 95 or Windows NT 4.0, a 100 MHz Pentium processor, 16MB RAM, and 10MB hard disk space. In addition, for video you'll need a digital camera and video capture card; and for audio you'll need a 16-bit sound card and drivers, in addition to a microphone and speakers.

● Go to http://support.cuseeme.com for information on compatible digital cameras.

2 If your system meets these requirements, cruise on over to the CU-SeeMe Web site at http://www.cu-seeme.com and follow the hypertext links to download the demo.

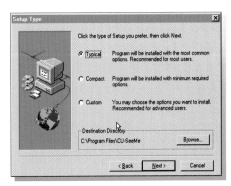

3 You have a choice of installation options. The typical installation should be right for most users.

4 The software will pour into your computer.

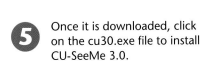

5 Once it is downloaded, click on the cu30.exe file to install CU-SeeMe 3.0.

How to Use CU-SeeMe

Okay, you have the software installed. Now it's time to get online and start communicating. This section will walk you through the basics of using CU-SeeMe.

1 Launch CU-SeeMe by clicking on the CU-SeeMe icon or file name in the folder of the same name.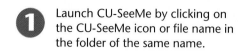

8 Once you are finished, you can hang up by clicking on the Hang Up button on the Conference Room toolbar.

7 You can choose from three types of conferences: Point to Point is your typical one-on-one "telephone" call. Group Conference requires a server that takes the input from many participants and distributes to all. Cybercast allows you to send your broadcasts to several recipients.

- If you right-click on a video portrait from the Conference Room, you can get the person's IP address so that you can establish a Point to Point connection.

- Don't worry about phoning in your PJs; you are never obliged to send video.

2 The program will ask you a few questions before entering the program proper. Note, it is *not* necessary to fill in all the personal information requested in order to use the software.

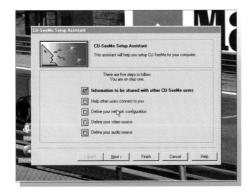

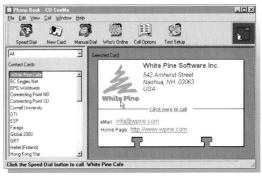

3 Once you have answered the questions to CU-SeeMe's satisfaction, you will be dumped into the Phone Book screen.

4 From the Phone Book you can place a call, test your setup, create a new card, or choose from several other options.

6 Once connected to another being, you'll be teleported to the Conference Room. This where you can see and talk to the person you have called.

5 There are three ways to place a call. To "phone" the person whose card is currently in the window, click on Speed Dial. To manually call someone, click the Manual Dial button and enter the person's IP address. To place a call to someone who is currently online, click the Who's Online button. A list of CU-SeeMe users currently online will scroll into the left pane. Select whom you wish to talk to and click the Speed Dial button.

How to Download and Install Voice E-Mail

Recently voice e-mail has been gaining popularity. The advantages are obvious: It takes less time to speak than type a message, you don't need to worry about spelling errors or punctuation with voice messages, and you can convey some of the warmth of your personality through your voice. The following pages demonstrate how to download, install, and use voice e-mail.

1 One of the best voice e-mail applications resides at http://www.bonzi.com/.

6 Voice E-Mail slaps these icons on your desktop when finished. The help file is helpful, so check it out. And the Player lets you listen to mail you receive (you can also do this from your Navigator window).

● Ensure you have the minimum requirements—most notably the 16-bit sound card, microphone, and speakers—before you download the software.

● There is no separate icon to launch Voice E-Mail. It is run from within Netscape.

2 When you arrive, you can choose either to download Voice E-Mail's player, which is free, or download the entire Send and Receive application for your specific platform.

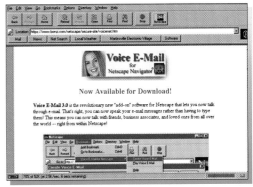

3 If you decide to download the full version, you will be whisked away to Voice E-Mail's secure page (note the key in the bottom-left corner), where you can transmit your credit card information.

4 Once the finances are taken care of, you can download Voice E-Mail 3.0.

5 Locate the folder that holds the downloaded file and double-click the file (vnsetup.exe). Voice E-Mail will unzip the file's contents and install the program.

How to Use Voice E-Mail

Voice e-mail truly is a convenience, not a trinket. Not only a time saver, voice e-mail provides that personal touch that helps in any business relationship. Although any e-mail routine has the capability to send attached .AVI files, Voice E-Mail uses a unique compression system that compacts and transmits voice e-mail in about the same amount of time as regular e-mail. These pages will show you how to make the most of it.

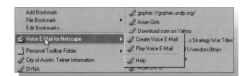

1 To create a voice e-mail message, click on the Voice E-Mail option under the Netscape Bookmarks menu.

● To include a picture, click the Insert button and select the file you wish to insert. Voice E-Mail handles nearly all popular image file formats.

● You can edit your e-mail and even add sound effects.

● Check out the variety of options on the Effects and Edit drop-down menus.

2 Next, click on Create Voice E-Mail.

3 Enter the e-mail address and subject as you normally would. You can still use your address book in the usual manner.

4 Now, rather than typing the text of your message, click the record button and speak.

5 Once you are finished, click the Send button and you are off to the races.

6 To listen to received voice e-mail, click the attachment link. Voice E-Mail will uncompress the file and play it.

INDEX

Numbers and Symbols

@ symbol, in e-mail addresses, 12
# (number symbol), 10
/ (forward slash), 11, 88

A

Acrobat Reader. *See* Adobe Acrobat Reader
Active Desktop, Internet Explorer 4.0, 200–201
ActiveMovie. *See* Microsoft ActiveMovie
ActiveX controls, Internet Explorer, 30
address book, e-mail, 12–13
   storing addresses, 142–143
Adobe Acrobat Reader, downloading, 113
All-Internet shopping site, 123
Alta Vista, 60
   using, 68–69
America Online (AOL)
   connecting to Internet through, 32–33
   dialing in to, 34–35
   gaming sites, 174
   using AOLNetFind, 72–73
anchor names, in URLs, 10
AND operator, 59
anonymous FTP. *See* FTP (File Transfer Protocol)
answering e-mail messages, 144–145
AOLNetFind, using, 72–73
attached documents
   adding to e-mail messages, 146–149
   compressing in ZIP files, 148–149
   receiving and saving, 150–151
audio controls, in Internet Explorer, 30
avatar, creating, 173
AVI files, 52

B

bandwidth, 4
Bess Web site, 129
bookmark folders, creating, 45
bookmarks
   adding to Internet Explorer, 46–47
   adding to Netscape Navigator, 44–45
   creating folders for, 45
   deleting, 44
   dialog box shortcut, 36
   organizing, 44–45
   shortcut key for adding, 36
   updating automatically, 48–49
Boolean operators, 59
boot-sector viruses, defined, 130
browsers. *See also* Microsoft Internet Explorer; Netscape Navigator
   defined, 6
   installing, 24–25, 28–29
   using, 37–55

C

caching of documents, 118–119
chain links, 39, 44
Chat 2.0 plug-in, 28
client/server relationships, defined, 6
Collabra, Netscape Communicator, 185
Comic Chat. *See* Chat 2.0 plug-in
CompuServe
   connecting to Internet through, 32–33
   dialing in to, 34–35
   game sites, 174
Composer, Netscape Communicator, 185
computer hardware, for Internet access, 18–19

connecting
    to FTP sites, 86–87
    to Internet via online services, 34–35
    to Telnet sites, 98–99
cookies
    getting comfortable with, 132–133
    options for in Netscape Communicator, 186
CoolTalk, 54
credit card purchases, on the Internet, 120–121
Ctrl+B, opening Bookmark dialog box with, 36
Ctrl+D, adding Bookmarks with, 36, 44
Ctrl+L, displaying Open Page dialog box with, 38
Ctrl+M, displaying mail composition window with, 134, 137
CU-*See*Me
    downloading and installing, 216–217
    using, 218–219
CuteFTP, 84, 90
CyberCash, shopping on the Internet with, 121
Cyber Patrol
    downloading and installing, 124–125
Cybernet, 125
CyberNOT list, 125

D

data transmission, 20–21
Deja News, 15, 158–159
DigiCash, 120–121
Digigami, Movie Screamer, 52
Digital Equipment Corporation, Alta Vista, 60, 68–69
digital IDs, 110, 116–117
discussion groups. *See* electronic mailing lists; newsgroups
document name, in URL addresses, 11
documents, attaching to e-mail messages, 146–149

domains, network, 13
downloading
    from FTP sites, 90–91
    installing software after downloading, 82–83
    software programs from the Internet, 80–81

E

Ecash, shopping on the Internet with, 120–121
electronic mailing lists
    choosing, 152–153
    finding out about, 152–153
    joining, 152–153
    list address vs. administrative address, 154
    overview, 152
    public vs. private, 155
    saving messages, 154
    subscribing to, 154–155
    unsubscribing from, 154
    viewing lists of lists, 118–119
Electronic Marketing Services, iMall by, 106, 123
Electronic Phone Directory, FreeTel, 55
e-mail
    addresses for, 12–13
    attaching files to messages, 146–149
    attaching ZIP files to messages, 148–149
    defined, 12–13
    forwarding messages, 144–145
    handling incoming messages, 140–141
    printing messages, 140
    replying to messages, 144–145
    saving and unzipping attachments to, 150–151
    sending from Internet Explorer 4.0, 30–31, 138, 206–207
    sending with Microsoft Exchange, 138–139
    sending from Netscape Communicator, 142–143

sending with Netscape Mail, 136–137

storing addresses, 142–143

unzipping ZIP files, 150–151

U.S. vs. international, 12

e-mail discussion groups. *See* electronic
mailing lists

Excite search engine, 83

EXE files, 59

F

FAQs (frequently asked questions), 164

Favorites list, Microsoft Internet Explorer

adding sites to, 31

updating automatically, 48–49

files

attaching to e-mail messages, 146–149

downloading from FTP sites, 90–91

uploading to FTP sites using Netscape, 85,
92–93

uploading to Web server using CuteFTP, 84,
90

file servers, defined, 3. *See also* Web servers

File Transfer Protocol. *See* FTP

file transfers. *See* downloading; uploading

file viruses, defined, 130

firewalls, 118–119

First Virtual, for shopping on the Internet, 121

flaming, defined, 164, 170

forums. *See* electronic mailing lists;
newsgroups

forward slashes (/), in URLs, 11, 88

frames, in Web pages, 42–43

Free Agent newsreader, 157

FreeTel, 54–55

frequently asked questions (FAQs), 164

FrontPad, Internet Explorer 4.0, 212–213

FTP (File Transfer Protocol)

addressing sites in URLs, 10

connecting to FTP sites, 86–87

downloading from sites, 90–91

logging in as anonymous user, 86

logging in to personal account, 86–87

navigating FTP sites, 88–89

overview, 84–85

saving files to disk, 91

uploading files to FTP sites, 85, 92–93

using CuteFTP, 84, 90

Web page links to sites, 7

G

<g> (grinning), 14, 170

Game Gateway site, 175

games

on the Internet, 174–175

joining online service for, 176–177

gateways, defined, 5

GIF files, 78

gopher

addressing sites in URLs, 10

overview, 102–103

printing documents, 104

saving documents, 104

visiting sites, 104–105

Web page links to sites, 7

Go To text box, 39

H

hardware, for Internet access, 18–19

hit list, 159

home pages. *See* Web pages

host computer, defined, 13

HotBot, using, 74–75

HTML (Hypertext Markup Language),
overview, 9

HTTP (Hypertext Transfer Protocol), 9

hyperlinks. *See* links

hypertext

defined, 8

links, 39

Hypertext Markup Language. *See* HTML
(Hypertext Markup Language)

Hypertext Transfer Protocol (HTTP), 9

I

Ichat, 168
image maps, defined, 39
iMall, 106, 123
Info*Seek*
    Free Software link, 66
    search engine, 61
    using search engine, 66–67
Integrated Services Digital Network (ISDN), 5,
    19
internal Webs, 119
Internet. *See also* World Wide Web
    background of, 3
    chatting on, 168–173
    connecting via Internet service providers,
        22–23
    connecting via online services, 34–35
    defined, 2–3
    gaming on, 174–177
    hardware for accessing, 18–19
    overview, 1–15
    protocol, 4–5
    security issues, 107–133
    shopping, 120–121, 122–123
    using, 77–105
    using for long-distance phone
        conversations, 54–55
Internet Explorer. *See* Microsoft Internet
    Explorer
Internet Mail, Microsoft Internet Explorer, 31
Internet News newsreader, 157
Internet phone software, 54–55
Internet Relay Chat (IRC). *See* IRC
Internet search engines, 58–59
Internet service providers
    connecting to Internet through, 34–35
    deciding on, 22–23
Internet Shopping Network (ISN), 122–123
Internet telephony, 54–55
intranets, 119

IRC (Internet Relay Chat)
    chatting with, 168–169
    chat etiquette, 170–171
    using voice-aided chat, 172–173
ISDN (Integrated Services Digital Network), 5,
    19
ISN. *See* Internet Shopping Network (ISN)
ISPs. *See* Internet service providers

J

JJ Electronic Plaza, 123
JPEG files, 78

K

kilobits per second (kbps), 21

L

LANs (local area networks), 3
links, 7
Listproc program, 154–155
Listserv program, 154–155
Liszt site, 152–153
local area networks (LANs), 3
Location text box, 39
Lycos search engine, 61
    Site Map, 64
    using, 64–65

M

Macintosh
    compression programs for, 150
    e-mail attachments for, 146
macro viruses, defined, 130
Mail Folder pane, Netscape Mail, 141
mailing lists. *See* electronic mailing lists
Majordomo program, 154–155
malls, online, 106, 122–123
McAfee's VirusScan for Windows 95, 130–131

Message Header pane, Netscape Mail, 140–141

Message pane, Netscape Mail, 141

messages, e-mail
  attaching files to, 146–149
  attaching ZIP files to, 148–149
  forwarding, 144–145
  handling incoming, 140–141
  printing, 140
  replying to, 144–145
  saving and unzipping attachments to, 150–151
  sending from Microsoft Internet Explorer 4.0, 30–31, 138, 206–207
  sending with Microsoft Exchange, 138–139
  sending with Netscape Mail, 136–137
  storing addresses, 142–143
  unzipping ZIP files, 150–151

Messenger, Netscape Communicator, 185

Microsoft Account Setup Wizard, 20

Microsoft ActiveMovie, 52

Microsoft Exchange
  address book, 142–143
  attaching files to e-mail messages, 146–147
  checking spelling in, 138
  forwarding e-mail messages, 144–145
  replying to e-mail messages, 144–145
  sending e-mail messages with, 138–139
  sending secure messages with, 114–115
  storing e-mail addresses, 142–143

Microsoft Internet Explorer, 6
  accessing newsgroups with, 208–209
  bookmarks, 46–47
  browsing offline with, 204–205
  configuring, 30–31, 202–203
  creating shortcuts in, 40
  displaying Web pages in, 38–39
  downloading, 194–195
  e-mail, 30–31, 206–207
  Favorites list, 31
  FrontPad, 212–213
  installing, 28–29, 196–197
  Internet News newsreader, 157
  Outlook Express, 206–207
  posting to newsgroups with, 210–211
  sending e-mail messages from, 138
  setup help page, 196
  shell integration, 198–199
  updating Favorites automatically, 48–49
  using Active Desktop, 200–201
  using other features of, 212–213

Microsoft Network
  connecting to Internet through, 32–33
  dialing in to, 34–35
  game sites, 174

Microsoft Plus, 28

mIRC, 169

modems, 5
  how they work, 20–21
  installing, 18–19

MOV files, 52

movies, watching on the Web with QuickTime, 52–53

Movie Screamer, 52

Mplayer gaming site, 174

MPG files, 52

MUDs, using, 178–179

N

navigation aids, finding, 60–61

Navigator. *See* Netscape Navigator

Netcaster. *See* Netscape Netcaster

net-filtering programs, 124–129

NetMeeting, Internet Explorer 4.0, 212–213

netiquette, 14, 170–171

Netscape Conference, 192–193

Netscape Communicator
  accessing newsgroups with, 190–191
  configuring, 186–187
  downloading, 182–183
  e-mailing with, 188–189

installing, 184–185

using other features of, 192–193

Netscape Mail

    address book, 137, 142–143

    attaching files to messages, 146–147

    deleting messages from, 140–141

    forwarding messages, 144–145

    launching WinZip automatically, 81

    printing messages, 140

    receiving messages, 140–141

    replying to messages, 144–145

    resizing window panes, 140

    sending messages, 136–137

    storing addresses, 142–143

    storing messages, 140–141

    viewing sent messages, 136

Netscape Navigator. *See also* Netscape Mail; Netscape News

    Account Setup Wizard, 29

    adding bookmarks, 44–45

    Chain Link button, 41

    configuring for Telnet, 96–97

    configuring, 26–27

    creating shortcuts in, 41

    disconnecting from, 24

    displaying Web pages in, 38–39

    and FTP sites, 90–93

    installing, 24–25

    navigating among Web pages, 40–41

    password setting in, 27

    setting options in, 26–27

    Web site address, 180

Netscape Netcaster, 48–49

Netscape News, 160–163

    resizing panes in, 160

    posting newsgroup messages, 166–167

    reading newsgroup messages, 162–163

    saving messages to disk, 162

Net Shepard, downloading and installing, 126–127

networks, defined, 2. *See also* Internet

newsgroups

    accessing with Netscape Communicator, 190–191

    accessing with Internet Explorer 4.0, 208–209

    addressing in URLs, 10

    defined, 14–15, 156–157

    etiquette, 14

    interacting with, 164–165

    moderated, 163

    participating in, 164–165

    posting messages, 166–167, 210–211

    printing messages, 14, 162

    reading messages, 30, 159, 162–163

    replying to messages, 166

    saving messages, 14, 162

    searching with Deja News, 14–15, 158–159

    subscribing to, 160–161, 191

    unsubscribing to, 160, 190

news host. *See* news servers

newsreaders

    Collabra, 190–191

    defined, 15, 157

news servers, 156

Norton AntiVirus, 106, 130–131

number symbol (#), 10

O

off-line browsers, 48–49

online malls, 105, 106, 120–121, 122–123

online services

    connecting to Internet through, 34–35

    dialing in to, 34–35

    installing, 32–33

OnLive! Traveler, 170–171

Open Page dialog box, Netscape Navigator, 38

OR operator, 59

Outlook Express, Internet Explorer 4.0, 206–207

    accessing newsgroups with, 208–209

    posting to newsgroups with, 210–211

P

packets, 5

passwords, 27

path, in URL addresses, 11

Peacefire anti-net-filtering Web site, 128

personal certificates, 110, 116–117

PGP software, downloading and installing, 112–113

plug-ins, 28

Point-to-Point Protocol (PPP), 22

pornography, software for blocking, 124–129

posting newsgroup messages, 166–167, 210–211

pound symbol (#), 10

PPP (Point-to-Point Protocol), 22

Pretty Good Privacy (PGP) software, 112–113

printing

    e-mail messages, 140

    newsgroup messages, 14, 162

    Web pages, 78–79

Prodigy, connecting to Internet through, 32–33

programs. *See* software programs

Progressive Networks Install Wizard, 51

protocols

    defined, 4–5

    Hypertext Transfer Protocol (HTTP), 9

    Point-to-Point Protocol (PPP), 22

    Secure Sockets Layer (SSL), 8

    Transmission Control Protocol/Internet Protocol (TCP/IP), 4–5

proxies, 118–119

Publicly Accessible Mailing Lists, 153

Q

QuickTime, 52–53

R

Rated-PG, 129

reading e-mail messages, 140–141

reading newsgroup messages, 30, 159, 162–163

RealAudio, listening to the Web with, 50–51

RealPlayer, 51

RealPlayer Plus, 50

RealVideo, 51

replying to e-mail messages, 144–145

replying to newsgroup messages, 166

routers, 5

S

saving

    e-mail messages, 150–151

    newsgroup messages, 14, 162

    Web pages, 78–79

searching newsgroups, 14–15

search routines, 59

search engines

    AltaVista, 60, 68–69

    Excite, 70–71

    Info*Seek*, 61, 66–67

    Yahoo!, 60, 62–63

search tools, finding, 60–61

Secure Electronic Transaction (SET), 120–121

secure messages, sending, 114–115

Secure Sockets Layer (SSL) protocol, 8, 108–109

Security Certificates, downloading and installing, 116–117

security issues, 108–109

    certifying Web sites, 116–117

    on the Internet, 107–133

    for organizations, 118–119

overview, 6

for parents, 112–113

visiting Web sites, 110–111

sending e-mail messages, 30–31, 136–139, 206–207

sending newsgroup messages, 166

Serial Line Internet Protocol (SLIP), 22

site certificates, 110–111

SiteMap, 64

SLIP (Serial Line Internet Protocol), 22

smileys, 165

software programs

downloading, 80–81

installing after downloading, 82–83

uninstalling, 82

spelling, checking in Microsoft Exchange, 138

SSL (Secure Socket Layer) protocol, 108–109

Starfish Internet Meter, 80–81, 82–83

status bar, 39

Stuffit, 150

subscribing to mailing lists, 154–155

subscribing to newsgroups, 160–161, 191

Surfbot 3.0, 48

SurfWatch, 129

T

TCP/IP (Transmission Control Protocol/Internet Protocol), 4–5, 33

TCP/IP stack, 5

telephone lines, 18, 19

TeleVox, 54

Telnet

addressing sites in URLs, 10

connecting to sites, 98–99

navigating at remote applications, 100–101

overview, 94–95

saving session contents to a text file, 100

using with Netscape, 96–97

threads, defined, 162

top-level domain, 12

Total Entertainment Network (TEN), 175

Transmission Control Protocol/Internet Protocol (TCP/IP), 4–5, 33

Tucows Web site, 157

2AM Games site, 175

U

uniform resource locators. *See* URLs

uninstalling programs, 82

unsubscribing from mailing lists, 154

unsubscribing from newsgroups, 160, 190

unzipping ZIP files, 150–151

uploading

to FTP sites, 85, 92–93

using CuteFTP, 84, 90

to Web servers, 226–227

URLs, 10–11. *See also* links

Usenet, defined, 156

Usenet newsgroups, reading with Internet Explorer, 30

user names, in e-mail addresses, 17

V

VeriSign, getting personal certificates from, 110, 116–117

video files, playing, 52–53

video formats, Internet Explorer, 30

video-conferencing software, 216–219

viruses

defined, 130

protective software, 130–131

VirusScan for Windows 95 (McAfee), 130–131

Voice e-mail

downloading and installing, 220

using, 222–223

VRML (Virtual Reality Modeling Language), 30

W

WANs (wide area networks), 3

WebCrawler, searching Web sites with, 58–59

Web movies, watching with QuickTime, 52–53

Web pages

creating shortcuts for, 40–41

displaying, 38–39

link overview, 6

navigating among, 40–41

order forms on, 6–7

printing, 78–79

saving, 78–79

Web search engines, 58–59

Web servers

addressing in URLs, 11

defined, 3, 6

Web sites, defined, 8, 9

Web Publishing Wizard, Internet Explorer 4.0, 22

WebTV, 214–215

Web Whacker, 48

wide area networks (WANs), 3

WinSock, 5

WinZip

attaching ZIP files to e-mail messages, 148–149

launching automatically from Netscape, 81, 150–151

saving and unzipping ZIP files, 150–151

Wizard, 149

World Wide Web. *See also* Web pages; Web sites

defined, 6–7

finding shopping areas on, 122–123

how it works, 8–9

listening to with RealAudio, 50–51

navigation aids, 60–61

searching, 57–75

search tools, 60–61

security issues, 120–121

Y

Yahoo!, 60

Internet shopping with, 122

using search engine, 62–63

Z

ZIP files

attaching to e-mail messages, 148–149

installing after downloading, 82–83

unzipping, 81